Dear Donna,
for the Grace Community
Library,

# AKUDRI

In His Joy
Pete & Edythe Broshar
Gal. 5:14

©Copyright 1990 by: Peter J. Brashler
All rights reserved.

Book Design by: Ryan Communications Group,
Marysville, WA

Library of Congress Catalog Number: 90-084783

ISBN: 0-9628119-0-4

Published By:
Cascade Publishing P.O. Box 1606 Marysville, WA 98270

Printed By: Eagle Graphics Co. Portland, OR

# AKUDRI

Africa Inland Mission
P.O.  Box 178
Pearl River, N.Y. 10965

# ABOUT THE AUTHOR

When Peter and Edythe Brashler sailed for the Belgian Congo in 1940 to work with Africa Inland Mission, they knew they were in for challenge and hard work. Yet no one anticipated the changes they would face in their more than thirty-five years there. Faith, patience, flexibility, and ingenuity were stretched to the limit.

Peter J. Brashler is a graduate of Biola College and has attended Everett (Washington) Community College and extension work with the University of Washington. For the final fourteen years of his service in Africa, he was Zaire (formerly Belgian Congo) Field Director. As a mark of the esteem in which he was held by the Zairian government, Brashler was awarded the prestigious Order of the Leopard, an honor accorded few white men. He is now Associate Pastor at First Baptist Church, Marysville, Washington and he and Edythe have recently celebrated their 51st wedding anniversary.

Their son Steve, joined his parents in Africa on their third term at the age of 1 and remained to graduate from Rift Valley Academy, Kenya.

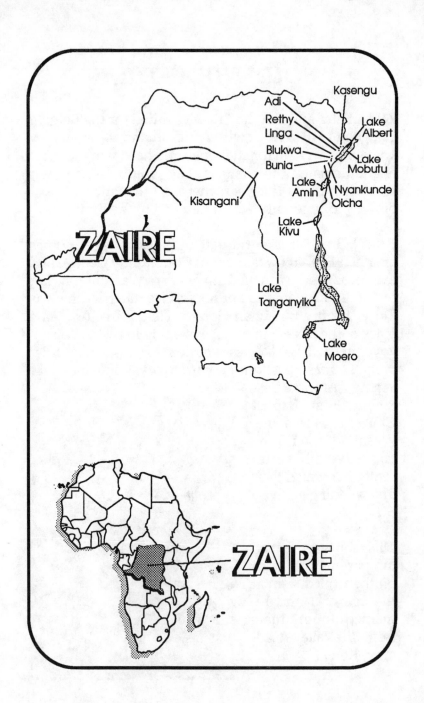

# *Foreword*

Most so-called "missionary" books see life in a developing country through the eyes of the foreigner.  It is refreshing to read a biography, which includes much missionary endeavor,  seen through the eyes of an African - an African of giant spiritual stature, yet so humble that he is glad to acknowledge his personal, and his national church's, debt to the foreign missionary, despite all the mistakes we have made.

As I read through the story as Akudri had related it, of his life as a youngster, a growing youth, a young man; of his transformation from paganism and fear of the power of the witchdoctor to Christianity and a personal faith in our Lord Jesus Christ; of his work as cook for his missionary friends to itinerant preacher all over the world - my heart was thrilled.  I have been taught so much in my own Christian life by African pastors of like godliness to Akudri.

Nearing the end, during the savagery of the "Simba Uprising" in the mid-sixties, his simply-told story brought back a flood of anguished memories - the brutality and senseless destruction, the fear and dread, the hammering on the door at the dead of night, and the raucous demand: "Open up, open up, in the name of the Army of Liberation!" and the wild mob who would rush in and ransack the house, stealing and smashing as they went.

How well I remember three such murderous men coming to the back door of my home one Sunday afternoon, demanding money.  I had none (and if I had had any, I would not have given it to them!).  "Liar!" they spat at me.

"Strike her down!" commanded the teenage leader. The soldier to my right raised his spear to drive it through me: another to my left intended to bring the butt end of his gun down across my head. I prayed for grace: I prayed to die from the first blow. Nothing happened. I raised my eyes, and saw both men 'fixed', unable to move, held as-it-were in the might grip of God. I nearly laughed! In my mind, I saw a Sunday School poster of Daniel, with his hands tied behind his back, in the den, encircled by a group of ravenous drooling lions - who could not touch him, because God had 'fixed' their jaws!

"My God in me is stronger than yours," I said. "Go round to the front of the house and I'll bring you coffee." I backed through the door, and slid to the ground, dizzy yet alive. God had delivered me once again.

As I read Pastor Akudri's story, I cried as he told of the same wonderful yet awful happenings. His story is true - I know it! I have been there, and proved the truth of the promise of the same wonderful God as he has done: "My grace is sufficient for you." God's grace is always sufficient for each one of us, in every need, every circumstance, every day, whatever it may be.

As you read this moving story of one of God's great gentlemen, may you be drawn closer to the Saviour, and be filled with the same great love that fills Akudri, and be sensitive to God's directing power into an ever-deepening commitment and loyalty in His service, as this gracious Pastor has so clearly demonstrated to us.

Helen Roseveare, MD
WEC International

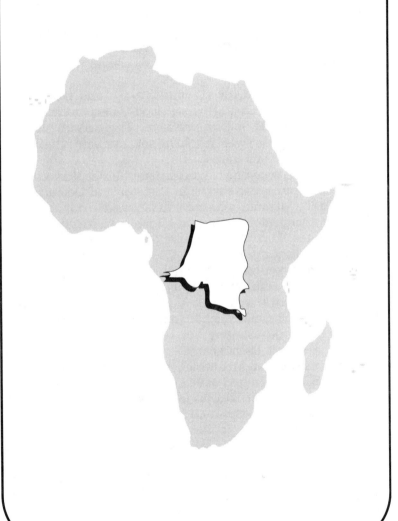

# THE SAGA OF YOANE AKUDRI
## Chapter 1
## Young Prophets and an Angel of Mercy

The fun fizzled out abruptly as machine gun fire began to bite into the hulk of the ungainly unimog. Thirteen young prophets and one seventy year old, venerable Pastor were travelling through Uganda in this army vehicle when it was ambushed.

The driver stopped the rig immediately, and they were surrounded by a menacing mob of blood-thirsty animals. No fair treatment could be expected here. This was Idi Amin's bailiwick, and these swashbuckling soldiers were remnants of his guerilla. They were killers.

"Out you get, everyone of you contemptible capitalists. In the name of our great sovereign Dictator and Defender of Allah's Faith, Idi Amin, we are commissioned to rid the earth of all the enemies of Allah, and all who are friends of the United States. Out with your hands on your heads, and kneel down on the ground."

The thirteen young evangelists had been having a blast. They had just completed a very successful evangelistic campaign in Kenya. Yoane Akudri had been appointed to be the leader of the pack. He had joined the young preachers in their boisterous singing but he did not share in their revelry. He had been scared, realizing that they were travelling through an area which was one of the last strongholds of the deposed and exiled Idi Amin. Yoane had been praying as the juggernaut jiggled noisily on its way. They had battled the neglected road for about 300 miles through Uganda, on their way to the Sudan to conduct another campaign.

Idi was a member of the same Kakwa tribe as Yoane was. This tribe was scattered through northwest Uganda and northeast Zaire, as well as in the Southern Sudan. Yoane's father bore the village name of "Dada" as did Idi Amin. Idi was a great leader of men, as was Yoane. Yoane had a voice like thunder, as did Idi. Yoane was a great leader who exuded charisma. Idi likewise oozed the same magic charisma. Both of these leaders were men of destiny - ordained to leave their mark in the history of Central Africa. The one great difference, however, was that Yoane was a servant of God, and Idi a servant of the devil. They were poles apart in their religious convictions, and they were both ready to die for their faith.

The menacing mob surrounding the unimog were thirsting for blood. No law and order could be expected here. The dozen or more barbarous buccaneers were all armed with machine guns. They were dressed in remnants of uniforms that had been stripped from their many victims. They brandished brazenly their weapons in the faces of the scared young preachers, threatening to kill them forthwith.

The rebels spotted Yoane amongst the younger men. Immediately they were suspicious of him, intuitively sensing that he was a man of strength, not unlike their own hero, Idi Amin. Their first impulse was to get rid of him - riddle him with machine gun fire. Why take any chances with this wily old wolf?

However, they were scared of Yoane. They would not want to be responsible for killing this old man of Nzambe (El Sheddai). Who could tell what kind of miraculous power this distinguished looking black man could call to his help? They would take him to the Rebel Colonel at Gulu.

"You too, M'zee," they said to Yoane, using the title of respect for a dignified old man. "You get out and join the young men. We want you to see them die. Then we will take you to Gulu to hear what the Colonel will do with you."

Yoane's joints were stiff from riding uncomfortably in the unimog. "Malamu" (O.K.), he replied, "but give me a little more time to get these old joints limbered up".

Yoane managed to extricate himself from the mean war machine. "So you are going to kill these young preachers are you? What kind of Africans are you? I've never seen an African executed without first having a fair trial. I don't believe that Idi Amin would ever approve of such injustice."

"Oh M'zee, you are wrong. This is Idi Amin's country, and all of these who deserve to die will first have a proper chance to defend themselves. We are Amin's men of justice. You are Christians. I can tell by your Bibles, and by the signs you have on your truck."

The leader of the group took charge of the formalities of the arrest: names, place of origin, destination, purpose of trip, and on. He wrote out a "warrant" for each one of them.

"Now, you prating preachers, you shall have a fair trial. What is the good of an execution without going through the theatrics of a court trial. We want to see you being tortured. We want to hear you beg for mercy. This will be a drama in real life, and much better than a television program. This will be like a carnival before the carnage feast."

The officer in charge commanded them all to get back into the unimog, along with an armed guard of six rebels. The chauffeur was ordered to drive them to Gulu.

It was dark when they arrived and the Colonel was already on his round of revelry. A contingent of heavily armed guards were assigned to guard the truck as the men slept on the ground under the vehicle. The trial was to be held the next day.

The night was a sleepless one for the prisoners. Morning came at long last, but not the Colonel. No trial. Guards were exchanged at 4 hour intervals. The preachers were glad for the reprieve, but they were scared.

"Cheer up." said Yoane, "these miserable monsters have no power over us unless it is given to them by God. We are in the hands of the Almighty. Come, you must be hungry. There's still some food in 'Goliata' (Goliath, their pet name for the giant war vehicle)."

Yoane found some parched corn in the vehicle, along with a basket of peanuts and a few sweet potatoes. It was cold and stale and unpalatable. They ate with very little relish. Their appetites had forsaken them along with their bravery.

"Tomorrow we will be shot!" one of them moaned. "Why doesn't God perform a miracle and get us out of here?"

This is how they all felt. They were all Christians, and assured of a happy home in heaven. They were not afraid to die, but they would just rather not be around when it happened.

Their worst problem was their thirst. As the chill darkness of the second night under the unimog engulfed them there was a noise of hungry hyenas lurking about to break the deadly silence.

"Those are the hellish hyenas, waiting for us to die," ventured one of the preachers. "They seem to know that we are going to be shot tomorrow."

"Will you pipe down," scolded another. "Why don't you go to sleep and forget your morbid mumbling. If we must die, we will die like men. Now be quiet and let us sleep."

Those were brave words that did not reflect the fear that gripped the heart of the speaker.

Crouching under the unimog with armed soldiers guarding them, the young men tried to sleep. One of them was heard snivelling. He tried to stifle his sobs under the rolled up jacket that was supposed to be his pillow. Others soon joined in the weeping. They did not want to die. They were young, and they had their wives and babies back in Zaire. Life might be tough in Zaire, but it was nothing like this. Grown men crying! This was too much for Yoane. His father-heart was broken too for Maria. It was 50 years ago that he had married his bride. How he would love to feel her tender embrace now.

"Khah! Khah!" Yoane said. "Why all this maimisu (water of the eyes)? Are we not men of strong faith in God? He will not allow the rebels' bullets to hurt us. They can kill our bodies, but so what? They will only open the door for us to enter that beautiful land where God lives."

Yoane began to extol the beauties of heaven. His eyes sparkled with glory as he spoke of the Savior. The old Septuagenarian preacher was able to allay the fears of the young prophets, like other young prophets of long ago that sat before Elisha, these watched the old Prophet restore the axe head of their faith. For the moment at least their courage was renewed.

The hunger, however, was gnawing at their inwards. When was the last time they had eaten a good meal. Their tongues were parched with thirst. Their hearts felt better, but their bodies were screaming for food and water. Could not the old prophet come up with another miracle?

Yoane had run out of miracles, but the God of miracles was still on the job. At 1:00 A.M. there was a snap of a twig. Could it be a soldier creeping up on them? Or was it a wild animal - a leopard? Or worse yet, a man-eating lion? One who was too old and stiff with arthritis to pursue his normal prey, and had turned to eating humans. These were much easier to pounce on.

The noise came nearer. Either a person or an animal was definitely approaching. "Mbote," whispered a cautious voice. "Do not be afraid. It is I, a Christian. I have come with food."

Yoane cautioned the young men. They must not awaken the guards. They would certainly kill the intruders, and perhaps the prisoners too. They crept silently from under Goliata, past the snoring guards, out to where the voice come from. The stars provided enough light to show them the timid little woman who was the angel of mercy. She was laying her life on the line to feed God's hungry prophets.

"My name is Dorcas", she whispered. "The Christians heard that you were being held captive, and that you were to be shot tomorrow. I prayed to Nzambe how I might help you. The first thought that came to me was your neglected stomachs. You must be hungry."

She had a large pot of steaming chicken - enough for generous helpings for all 14 of them. An earthen pot was filled with manioc mush. A complete dinner of savory gravy, hot vegetable greens and a good supply of roasted bananas. There was a large jug of hot coffee. All Africans like coffee. All except Yoane, but she also had a gourd full of fresh milk, and a supply of drinking water. That such a little slip of a woman could manage such a load through the darkness, and find her way to the hungry prophets, was truly amazing. Yoane whispered a prayer of thanksgiving. A short one because their gastric juices were salivating. "Please, God," he added, "keep the rebels from smelling this food, and keep them asleep while we eat."

They ate lustily, emphasizing the swallows by polite, but muffled burps, and contented sighs. They must show

Dorcas their appreciation by generous burps. Food that was eaten burplessly was not really fit to be eaten.

The angel of mercy slipped away with her empty containers as noiselessly as she had come. She promised to come again the next night. The soldiers had not awakened. The evangelists had another session of prayer and settled down on their grass mats under the unimog. They slept soundly but not soundlessly until the first roosters began to crow in the new day. The day that the Lord had made. Could they rejoice in it and be glad? Only God knew what was in store for them.

At 10:00 A.M. the officers arrived with a contingent of soldiers, heavily armed. The usual harassment followed: "Who are you? Where do you come from? Why are you here? Where are you going?"

Yoane, always the spokesman, answered the questions forth rightly and politely, but the rebels would not believe him. "Bah! - Ba Kristu," they gesticulated with profanity. So that's what you are - Christians. You are enemies of Allah, and friends of the hateful Americans! Exploiters of Africa. You want to eat up our country! We pray to Allah, and you hate Allah. You must die!" the officer screamed.

At this point Yoane broke the sound barrier with his trumpet voice, "You listen to us," he shouted. "We are God's messengers, and we are here on His business. We hate nobody, and we love the Nzambe whom you call 'Allah'. We are here to tell you that you are sinners, and that the wages of sin is death. Unless you repent you will be banished from God's presence for all eternity. We have our passports in order, and our travel documents. You can kill us if you want to, and we will go directly to heaven. But you will just add 14 more murders to your sinful records. You shall have to answer to Allah for that."

The swashbuckling soldiers were taken aback. Who was this dignified looking old man who would dare to speak to Amin's officer like this? He sputtered, "You listen to me, M'zee (old man), you are very bad to talk like that. You, and all these whimpering upstarts will be shot tomorrow. We shall see who is going to be banished."

The trial was over. The sentence was passed, and would be summarily carried out the next day. The guards over the prisoners were doubled, and the officers left in a huff. The young men began to sob again. This broke Yoane's heart. He was not afraid for himself, he had faced death many times.

"Aoki kwanza (listen to me)," Yoane began, "God is in control. If God has a work for us then the rebels are powerless. Think of Daniel in the lions' den. God closed their mouths so that Daniel could sleep right beside them. In the morning God delivered Daniel. Think also of Shadrak, Mesaka and Abedenego. They were handcuffed, and shackled, and thrown into the raging furnace. God walked with them in the fire and allowed only their fetters to be touched by the flames. They came out of the furnace without even the smell of smoke on them. Think of Peter in the bloc. God was there in the prison with him. He opened up a free path for him. The same Nzambe is right here with us. I believe He will deliver us. I really believe that."

The young men were not to be placated. The execution was scheduled, and they were horrified. The thought of bullets ripping through their bodies was too much for them.

Late in the afternoon a car drove up, and a nicely dressed black woman stepped out. She greeted Yoane by name, but the Pastor did not recognize her. "My husband knows you. I am the wife of the Askofu (Bishop)," the lady said. "I am going to try to help you. I am going to talk to the rebels in charge here. I am on my way to Nairobi, and I shall do what I can for you. God is able."

Yoane scribbled a note to Vickie Paul, his evangelist Coordinator in Nairobi, explaining the situation to him. This he gave to this second angel of mercy to deliver. She called on the rebel officers that evening.

"You better not hurt these men of God or the whole population will rise up against you. You must keep them alive until we can contact your superiors in Kampala." With more convincing, and some cajoling, the woman impressed the rebels. They decided to wait for orders from Kampala. The Bishop's wife went to Nairobi and delivered Yoane's letter. Several days later the prisoners were free. They did not, however, leave the rebels in Gulu without a clear witness concerning Who Jesus Christ is, and what He can do for sinners who will trust Him. The freed captives continued their journey to Sudan. The 13 young evangelists were strengthened in their faith. The seventy year old pastor added yet another saga to his remarkable life's story. The pages that follow are a narrative of the life of this hero of the faith, and the unique ministry that God has accomplished through him.

"Having quenched the violence of fire, and having escaped the edge of the sword," this old soldier went on to continue his good fight, and to finish his course with joy and much laughter, as well as many tears.

The following pages will relate the story of his long life of service for God. ❖

Edythe & Peter Brashler
on their 50th Wedding Anniversary

Pete & Edythe with their son, Steve, in Adi, Zaire
*Photo by J. Copeland*

## Cheating His Brother's Grave
## Chapter 2

Yoane will never forget the year of the "Walking Sickness". It was after he had lived through about eight dry seasons. He could never be sure of his exact age because the Kakwa tribe had no way of keeping birth records.

However, they do remember great calamities and chronology is based on these. One would never forget the rainy season when the earth went into a frenzy and began to dance. That earthquake swallowed whole rows of huts down into the mammoth maw of the earth. Giant trees were uprooted by the angry spirits that kept their abode underneath the torrential Nzoro River. More people died than could be counted on all the fingers and toes of the whole clan.

Such an event would be remembered by passing on the story to their children from one generation to the next. History was recorded by the number of dry-seasons following a particular disaster until the next one should come along, be it fire or flood, famine or fateful disease.

Yoane was charged with emotion as he recalled and relived the horrible dry season of the Walking Sickness (spinal meningitis).

"It was that moon," Yoane explained, "when the rains refused to come and wash the earth. The hot winds were on a rampage, like a swarm of yelling yellow jackets. All the streams were dried up like the last drops of water in a boiling pot that had stayed on the fire too long. Many people died of thirst."

Yoane paused to reflect as he relived those horrendous days. "Was that a longer and more difficult dry season than usual?" we asked. We had come specifically from Everett, Washington to hear and record these stories of his life, and we wanted to get the details.

"Oh yes, much longer. The tall grass had withered and bent over like a tired old woman who had carried too many loads of manioc flour on her head. The air was dry and hot like the heat waves blown over our village from the grass fires that scorched the fields. The sun hid its face behind the clouds of dust that came lower and lower each day until they finally dropped their powder on the earth. The gardens had all burned to a crisp. Our bellies began to growl like the starving leopard growls angrily at the hyenas lurking nearby, waiting for the leopard to die. Our whole village was crying, and begging the spirits for the water they were withholding. Like a starving baby nuzzling his mother's shrivelled breasts, trying to coax that last drop of milk that is no longer there, our people were dying of thirst."

Yoane was working up more and more emotion as he talked to us. "Were you old enough to remember all the details?" we queried.

"I remember very clearly, Bwana, just like it might have been last dry season. I can still feel the hunger after all these years. Not only were we hungry and thirsty, but many of our tribe began to get sick with the sickness that walks. It steals from hut to hut, and village to village, pouncing on its helpless victims like an old man-eating lion. It ravages and destroys, eating some of its prey, and leaving other mangled victims for the hyenas."

Yoane paused, pensively reliving those days. "Soon the walking sickness visited our hut, attacking my older brother."

"How did it affect him?" we asked.

"It dried up all the liquids of his body, and burned inside of him like a fiery torch. My brother had a very strong physique. He could follow a wounded buffalo a whole day without stopping to eat or drink. He fought valiantly to conquer this wild beast, the walking sickness. After only two sunsets his body succumbed to the devastation of this disease, and his spirit was carried away by the spirits of our ancestors."

"How dreadful! Were you afraid, Yoane, that you too might be carried away?"

"Oh yes, Bwana, we were all afraid. My father called the 'Nganga na Bashenzi' (witch doctor) because our ancestors' spirits had been seriously offended, we thought. They were taking out their vengeance on us.

"After the burial of my brother the Nganga gathered all of my uncles and aunts and cousins into the libanda (court yard), and had them all sit in a circle."

"Did he have all of his paraphernalia with him to divine what it was that caused the sickness?"

"Oh yes, he had a basket full of chicken claws, a collection of monkey paws, rat tails, snake heads, gourds filled with dried beans, antelope skins, leopard fangs, guinea fowl feathers, and on and on. The smell of this collection forced its way into our nostrils, trying hard to make us vomit."

"I thought you Africans didn't mind putrid smells."

"Our noses may not be as sensitive as yours," retorted Yoane, "but that witch doctor with his charms was something else. His odor could penetrate the hot dry season wind so that you could smell him a mile away, even if he was down wind from you.

"He was dressed in a leopard skin, and wore an old manioc basket as a hat on his lice-infested kinky head. The hat was decorated with feathers of the most colorful, exotic birds. He had a whistle which he blew sharply in his divination ceremonies as he beat his small drum.

"He also had a gourd full of human fingernails which he had extracted from some of his hapless victims. He believed that in these fingernails there was a special charm that gave him power to divine secrets of the spirit world. All of our people felt there was real 'soul-value' in the human fingernails. The witch doctor paid a great price for them."

Yoane saw that he had a very interested audience in Edythe and me. He warmed up to his story.

"After we were all seated, about 35 in our clan - he asked for a live rooster. We boys had to chase through the hot sun to catch the scared old bird. It seemed that even the rooster knew there was a bad omen awaiting him. "When the nganga finally got his gnarled fingers around the neck of the fowl, he had us all sit close together in a circle. With his razor sharp knife he cut the chickens head off with one clean stroke. He threw the writhing bird on the ground in the center of the circle.

"The rooster danced round and round in a convulsive,

quivering manner, writhing and squirting blood on all of us. Finally the convulsions became weaker, and the proud old cock of the walk slumped in a dead heap of feathers and tough chicken meat."

"Yuckie" responded Edythe. Yoane hadn't a clue as to what "Yuckie" meant so he continued his story.

"The headless neck of the rooster was pointing directly at one of my favorite uncles. The nganga summoned this Uncle to him, claiming that the decapitated bird had accused him of offending the evil spirits."

"My Uncle denied any complicity with the nasty little demons, but the nganga tried to force a confession out of him. When the Uncle refused to confess the witch doctor began to beat him with a sturdy stalk of elephant grass. That was the signal for the whole clan to get into the act. They must punish this uncle even though he was very popular in the whole clan. If necessary they would kill him."

"Did the Kakwas actually sacrifice a person's life in such a demoniac orgy as this?"

"Oh yes, Bwana. Some dry seasons prior to this the Bulamatadis (Belgian Officials) arrived to take control of our country, and they did not approve of this procedure. They tried to stop it, but the Kakwas continued doing it secretly. Whenever the Belgians discovered a village sacrificing a person they would make all the men of the village lie down on their bellies, bare bottoms up. The soldiers whipped each one severely with a hippo-hide whip, ripping their buttocks and thighs into shreds until they looked like a leopard had clawed them.

"Now, instead of killing the victim who had the misfortune of a headless rooster-neck pointing in his direction, they beat him mercilessly, and sent him off into the forest. There he must live like an animal until finally he falls victim to a rapacious predator who subsists on the carnage of the weak."

"Did the Kakwas actually believe that the witch doctor had power to stop such an epidemic?" queried Edythe.

"Oh yes, the wicked old nganga cast a very powerful spell over all our people during those days, even though he was not able to stop the walking sickness. A few days after the witch doctor drove my Uncle into the forest my mother died.

"He told us not to worry about my mother because her breasts were all dried up like an old ear of corn that had remained on the stalk too long. She would not be able to bear any more children."

"What kind of a woman was your mother?"

"She was a very kind person. She told us many stories of the past as we sat around the fire in the evening. She and we children did not eat with the men. They had important things to talk about that were not meant to be heard by female or children's ears. Two days after my mother's death my father, Dada, died. This caused great mourning because he was the head man of the village. The whole clan, indeed, the whole village gathered in our libanda (court yard) to dance through the whole night. They drank gallons of potent beer, and distilled liquor that made them dance like the rooster that had lost its head.

"Not only did they drink and dance, but the wailed at the top of their voices, thinking the confusion would drive the spirits away. Both men and women carried sharp knives at their waists. With these they carved ugly gashes all over their bodies. If they could have found water they would have made mud to plaster their faces and bodies. Because of the drought they had to be satisfied with writhing in the dust.

"But all of this did not stop the walking sickness. The disease walked into my sister's hut and she too died the same day. We were too exhausted to shed many tears over her. After all, we thought, she's only a female, and soon she would be sold to another clan to become the wife of a stranger. Too bad to lose the dowry price she would have brought, but there were more important things to worry about.

"The next day my last brother died. That meant my father, Dada, and my mother, my brothers and my only sister were dead. Graves had been dug and filled for each of them except my last brother. His body was lain in the grave, but they were too tired to fill the excavation. I was the only one left of our immediate family." "You must have felt awfully alone,

Yoane," we sympathized, "what did you do?"

"Before my relatives had filled my last brother's grave, the walking sickness grabbed my body. I was the last one of Dada's children. The uncles and aunts were tired of digging new graves. They decided to keep this grave open until the spirits would carry away my spirit. Then they would place my body on top of that of my brother.

"Some of the villagers spread the word that Akudri was very sick. 'Akudri' is the name Dada gave me when I was born. It means 'Latecomer', and they called me that because I lingered long inside my mother's belly. I had arrived about ten suns later than I should have. I was appropriately named, 'Akudri', the dawdler."

"My uncles laid my withered body on a mat under the shade of the veranda of Dada's hut. Nobody came near me to cry over me. Had my mother been there, she would not have been afraid of my sickness. She would have held me in her arms, and would have chanted songs to the spirits to soothe them, and to entice them to go away. She would have taken her knife and carved many little ditches on my belly and on my forehead to let the sickness run out of my body with the flow of blood through the ditches."

"Oh Yoane," exclaimed Edythe, "that's cruel. How could your mother do that to you?"

"She would have done all that, thinking she was doing the right thing. She would have mixed a poisonous potion of dawa (medicine) and forced it down my throat. However, she had already joined the spirit world, along with all the rest of my family. There was no one left to dance over me, or to wail away the evil spirits. I was left to find my own way into the spirit world.

"The likondos (evil spirits), however, are very fickle. My body was left lying on the veranda the whole day and through the night. I had already joined the spirit world, but the spirits decided they did not want me. They sent me back to Akudri's body, and I was very sick for a few days."

"My uncle became impatient with me. He wanted to fill the open grave of my brother's body. What if the Bulamatadis would come and find the open grave with my brother's body swelling and smelling like the putrefaction of death. They wanted to throw me into the grave and get the job finished."

Yoane stopped to wipe his brow. He pondered a moment as the panorama of that horrible moment flashed before him. "But one of my uncles insisted that my spirit had returned to my body. He found water enough to dampen a cloth and wash my face and my arms. He gave me a few drops of the precious liquid to cool my parched tongue.

"Gradually I became stronger. Someone came with a gourd of goat's milk and forced some of it down my throat. I lingered for days, and finally my uncles had to fill my brother's grave. The spirits had refused me.

"All the villagers were amazed. I had come back from the world of spirits. They decided that there was a special work for me to do. Maybe I would become the head of the clan. Or perhaps I would become the leader of the dance. I had always had a strong voice that could be developed into one like a lion's voice. I had always been noted for my lithesome limbs and for the kind of rhythm that should be the quality of a dance leader.

"They decided to nourish me well to help me regain my good health. They would teach the arts and secrets of being a village Kapita (leader). I would be the head man."

"Who was to be the head man in the place of your father?" we asked.

"Dada's oldest brother, named Tata, became the next head of the clan. He also became my father, and he treated me as one of his own sons."

Yoane continued his chronicle after we had stopped for a cup of tea. He was anxious to get on with the story.

"Soon after my whole family had died, and I had cheated my brother's grave, the lightning began to flash. The thunder growled like an old lion who had succeeded in killing a water buck. The dust filled the sky that had been hidden from the sun for many days. The air was stifling and humid. The midday had become a menacing black."

"The wind became very angry and tore much of the thatch off of our huts. It chased the dust away in great clouds, making it hard for us to breath."

"The dust was followed by great drops of water that was lapped up by the dust that covered the parched earth. The rain descended in a torrential deluge that lasted for about one hour. The water on the libanda (court yard) became a large lake. Water, water spread out everywhere.

"The wind began to get tired. Finally it stretched and yawned, and lay on the ground. The gentle rain continued for about another hour before it finally eased off. The clouds broke open and ran in every direction. The sun, that beautiful light that Nzambe had given us, burst through the clouds. The earth was washed clean, and the river beds were no longer dry. The drought was over, and Nzambe was happy again. The ugly spirit of the walking sickness had left us."

"Yoane, when the epidemic left your village what did the people do to get back to normal life again?"

"Many days of dancing followed the walking sickness", Yoane continued. "The Nganga stayed for many days to rebuild the spirit house so that we could again offer our regular sacrifices.

"Each day we would have to kill a goat or a sheep until all of our herds and flocks were almost exhausted. I used to grumble about the waste of good goat or cow meat being used in these sacrifices. Tata, however, reminded me that he was an authority on spirit worship. We must do nothing to offend them. But still, I thought to myself, I would rather roast these chickens, and barbecue these sheep for a good feast. I would take my chances with the spirits. Hadn't I cheated them once, and couldn't I do it again!

"In addition to the meat sacrifices there were also the libation offerings of large quantities of beer being poured out by the witch doctor before the spirits. The nganga drank gallons of the potent brew, which, he claimed, was all for the purpose of worshipping the spirits.

"The dancing went on for weeks amidst wailing and shouting and drinking fiery liquor. Night after night the ceremony went on, which in reality was nothing more than a drunken orgy."

Yoane had finished the chronicle of the sickness that

walks, and the effect that it had on their family. He cannot talk about it without praising God for delivering him and his people out of such pagan bondage. He no longer attributes their deliverance to the witch doctor.

He knows that God had a wise plan in mind for him when he was saved from his brother's grave. This great apostle and evangelist, whom his father called "Akudri", the "late comer" because he dawdled inside his mother's womb, was later to be widely known on four different continents.

He was to become an Apostle of God's grace, and like John the Baptist, after whom he was later named, he would preach the Gospel of Repentance. Like John the Apostle, he would become a Father in the Lord to multitudes of christians whom he would teach, "My little children, these things write I unto you that ye sin not." ❖

Pigmies at Maitulu where Akudri preaches

Mr. & Mrs. Bell

## Growing Pains
## Chapter 3

Yoane's recovery from meningitis was a slow and painful process. For weeks his appetite was poor, having no palate for the unsavory fufu that was his daily diet. Only rarely was he given a few spoons of chicken broth, or a morsel of meat. These he ate with relish, but it took him a long time to generate a good appetite.

His legs were like sticks of bamboo, and his body like a walking skeleton that was flabbily wrapped in leathery skin. His eyes were deeply sunken into their sockets, and one could easily trace the contours of a face-less skull. He had cheated his brother's grave once, but it looked like the grim reaper was still hard on his trail.

Gradually, however, his desire for food came back to him. His taste for fufu was still rather "blah", but bananas, peanuts, some of the nectarous fruits of the forest, and some morsels of chicken and broth were all taken with relish. With his increased appetite gradually his strength returned. And with his strength his mischievous delight in being alive. His uncle, who was now his father, and whom Akudri called "Tata", often referred to his new son as "Mototo na Yawili", being "The child of mischief." He truly delighted in teasing his sisters and brothers, even old Tata himself was not exempt from his pranks. Tata's immediate family were smiled upon by the spirits. Not one of them had died in the walking sickness. He had married a second wife several years before the epidemic, so there were two wives to bear children for him. He had no trouble in keeping them periodically pregnant, and his family was proliferating like a flock of sheep.

Two of the wives, however, complained about the heavy volume of work they had to do. They got along surprisingly well with each other, dividing the work between them evenly. But still, they felt that Tata was unfair with them. They decided to do something about it.

"Tata", they taunted him, "What is this with you? Are you

weaker than the other men? Most men have three or four, or even five wives, and you have only two. Is it that you are less of a man than they? You must be a slacker, or you too would have more wives."

This was too much for Tata - calling him a slacker! Even implying that he was impotent. He beat them severely until the lashes created rivulets of blood that flowed off their buttocks. He had to teach these two hateful heifers a lesson they would not forget.

Then he began to negotiate immediately with one of his neighbors for his sixteen year old daughter called Kitoko (the beautiful one). The price was too high - four cows and ten goats -but he agreed, and all but depleted his wealth in order to pay the dowry. He would show his wives whether he was impotent. Now he had three wives. That would generate even more babies, and keep the recalcitrant ones out of mischief by making more work.

The first two wives were still in disgrace, and their lacerated limbs were still quite painful, but they were extremely happy. They had inveigled Tata into acquiring a third wife who would become their servant. The beating and the temporary disgrace was well worth the luxury of having Kitoko as their servant. She may be the favorite of Tata, and be able to share his sleeping mat, but she would have to bear the brunt of the work. And Tata had not discerned the plot. He would soon have the little Kitoko hussy pregnant and then he would call for his old faithfuls again.

Akudri, however, was not fooled by the deceit of his two aunts, and with great amusement he watched the drama unfold. Tricking the old Tata was extremely funny to him. In fact, he too got into the act.

"Ah, Tata", he exclaimed, "now you have three wives. But you just wait until I have found the full virility of my body. I will make you look like the runt of a litter of Bashenzi Pups. You have three wives. I shall have six. I shall be twice as important as you, with twice as many children. Then you will appear as an impotent old bull buffalo in the eyes of your wives."

Tata didn't know what to make of the threat. He should

beat this Yawili son of his, and teach him not to be impudent. But the young boy had developed into a fine looking, strong athletic person. He regarded this son of his brother as one who had come out of his own loins. And the attraction was mutual. Akudri too liked his new father, Tata, even though he was amused at his gullibility in letting his two wives trick him.

Akudri's body developed into that of a strong athletic man. He could endure through long hours of a blistering-hot day out on a hunt. He was agile, able to scale the height of the tallest mahogany trees in order to spy on a herd of buffalo and send signals to the hunters below. He could run like a young gbodi (bush buck), and he could track a wounded animal even better than their bashenzi dogs.

When neighbors encroached on his garden space, or quarrelled about boundaries, Akudri could out-talk any of them with his loud voice, and bluff them into a good settlement for Tata. Given a few more years to find his full body, he would certainly become the head of the clan, indeed, the whole village.

Akundri's excellence outshined in the dance. He was of lithesome limb, and limber as a lizard, going through all the contortions with perfect rhythm. His trumpet voice could call out the dance signals with the voice of a lion so that the whole village could hear. He had the strength to endure through the whole night and on through the next day. All of his family, even the newly-acquired Kitoko, who was only a few years his senior, voted that Akudri was to be the leader of the dance. The spirits had decreed this, and he was a man of destiny.

To become such a person he must also have the appearance of a dancer. He must wear anklets of copper bands with tiny bells attached. He must have metal rings in his ears, also with tiny bells attached so that as he danced he could make the jingle-bell effect. His strong young body must have the right tatoo markings. This meant that sizable holes had to be pierced in his ear lobes. How else could the ear bells be attached?

The ears were pierced and the metal forced through the

wounded lobes and fastened with copper wire. They looked great and the sound effect of the bells was perfect, but Akudri wondered how he was going to endure the pain.

As the little finger-nail shaped ring of the new moon appeared at about sundown, Akudri started his first dance. It was a tremendous success. The villagers, under their new leader cavorted, and cut every conceivable kind of caper all through the night. What an orgy they enjoyed as they slithered and slurped their potent masanga (beer). He continued relentlessly with the frenzied frazzle of men on into the next sun. They shouted with the nzenzes (native guitars). Yoane's mettle was tested but he passed the test to everyone's delight. He was the king of the dance.

But what about his sore ears? They were bleeding profusely, and the perspiration exuding freely from his grimy hair and face mingled with the blood. Kitoko, who looked more like his sister than his step-mother came with a pot of boiling water and, with a little gourd she poured the scalding liquid on his wounded ears. The pain excruciating, but it did seem to prevent infection. But these wounds were to be reckoned with years later. They played a very important role in God's sovereign plan for his life.

When Akudri was about fourteen dry seasons old, word came to Tata's village that a mondeli (white man), and his Madame were going to visit Kakwa land. Many of the older men had gone to Chief Drupa's village when the Belgian officials visited the area, but none of the younger generation had ever seem a white man. In fact, they doubted that there could be such a person. Old Tata was trying to deceive them. Did Nzambe (God) not create all men black? These so-called mondeles (white men) must have some of that whitewash, that the Kakwa call pembe, all over their bodies. They were not about ready to swallow this story. Akudri told Tata that he didn't believe a word of this stuff about a "white man".

"Very well", replied Tata, "you shall go with me to Kukalunga where this man is supposed to arrive and you shall see with your own eyes."

Father and son set off to Kukalunga the next morning before the first roosters began to crow in the new sun. They wanted to be there in plenty of time for his arrival. About noon the Kukalunga drums began to cry, and the men began to sing "Mondeli sirayii!" (white man has arrived). The whole village ran out to meet him. Finally a strange looking, rather slight man appeared, followed by a long row of carriers with bundles on their heads. A little farther down the line of procession were four husky blacks carrying a tepoy, the same kind of a carrying chair that was used for the chief when he went on a long safari. In the chair was a white woman, the wife of the Mondeli. What peculiar people they were. Their hair was straight instead of the kinky kind that Nzambe put on black people's heads. And they both had a straight path running right down their hair from the front to the back. Akudri had the answer to that strange phenomenon. It must be a path they cut for the fleas to walk through.

"Look at their noses!" exclaimed another. "Nzambe certainly had a strange pattern from which He made these mondelis. Who ever saw such long and pointed noses?" Later they noticed that they both had a cold, and that they put their nose into the cloth and pulled their noses to wipe them dry. They concluded that that was the reason they had such long noses - they were always pulling at them with the little white cloth.

But these two white people, whom they learned to call Bwana and Madame Bell, were very friendly. The Bwana had a gold tooth in the front of his mouth which flashed brightly when he smiled, which was very often. The flashy tooth caused much amazement, and was discussed long into the night. Akudri thought that Tata would look very nice with such a mark of distinction. One morning they peeped into the hut which was provided for the visitors and they saw the Madame combing her hair. "Kah! Kah! Kah!" they exclaimed. "Her hair reaches all the way down to her hips! What strange people, but ever so friendly."

Bwana and Madame Bell spoke to the leading men of the village in Bangala. This was the trade language which the Kakwas used officially with the Belgian Officials, and also when they negotiated with other tribes who did not speak Kakwa. As the missionaries spoke to the Kakwa people in

Bangala, one of the younger and better educated men interpreted their messages into the tribal language. But Madame was not happy with this arrangement. She asked the men to say certain words in Kakwa, and she would imitate them. The Kakwas were convulsed in laughter when they heard this white-skinned woman, with hair that reached down to her hips, speaking phrases in the Kakwa's vernacular.

"Oyo-azi nini? (What is this)" the missionaries learned to say, as they pointed to various objects. Soon they were able to use some very simple phrases, and the women particularly were absolutely enamored with this woman that must have come from another planet.

The Bwana came out every morning with a strange looking black object. "Oyo azi nini?" queried one of the Kakwas, pointing to the strange object." "Oyo azi book" replied the Bwana, not knowing what the name would be in Bangala.

"Buku", as they pronounced it, meant nothing to the Kakwas because they had never seen one. Mr. Bell opened the book and showed them the printed pages that to them looked like the tracks of a crow on a newly planted garden. "But what is it?" persisted the villagers. "What is its work?" "This Buku." responded the missionary, "is the Word of Nzambe. It contains all his instructions, and everything He wants to say to us. It tells us that Nzambe created us as "Batu Bipuru" (people that are clean of all sin), "and that He loves us."

"But we know that", responded old Tata. "We know that Nzambe has created us, and that everything good comes from Nzambe. The sunshine, the rain; our gardens that grow; our wives that bare children; our healthy bodies. All that is good comes from Nzambe." They had a piece of common ground from which to start. Both blacks and whites had a healthy respect for Nzambe, the Lord of the earth. They were very intrigued with the stories of the "Buku", which they now called the "Monoko na Nzambe" (Word of God). But how could one ever learn the meanings of all those crow tracks on the pages? Certainly these must be magic, or some spirit-formula whereby they too could learn what those strange looking marks were saying. Mr. Bell patiently answered their questions, and spent hours each day talking about the Nzambe they knew as Creator, but nothing about His plan of redemption.

The next day he went a step further with God's truth. He showed them the pages of Genesis three, and began very simply to explain the history of Adam and Eve's sin of disobedience. He told them about the serpent that loaned his beautiful body to Jaboro, the hateful enemy of Nzambe. This character was no stranger to the Kakwas. They spoke very softly when they discussed Jaboro because they did not want the wicked spirits to hear what they were saying. If they knew that the Kakwas were talking to the strange Mondele about Jaboro, they would surely punish them by sending another catastrophe like the walking sickness. Perhaps something even worse.

Bwana and Madame stayed many days with the Kakwas. Akudri was the right-hand man, and was extremely interested in all the proceedings. Old Tata was a bit afraid, and he felt he should call the witch doctor to make some sacrifices to the spirits. To provide for this would be a costly thing, at least a dozen chickens, several goats and a sheep. It would be worth it, however, not to take any chances in offending the spirits again. A sort of insurance policy. He wasn't quite sure where he would get the animals and birds for the sacrifices because his own flocks were depleted after marrying his third wife, Kitoko. He would ask his relatives to help him.

Tata decided it was time to go back home. He was getting anxious to see Kitoko again, and also those other two conniving cronies. He had forgotten about how they had insulted him. He would go to Kitoko's hut first, but after several days he would also visit the other stinkers. He must get his safari gear wrapped immediately so he and Akudri could go home.

"But Tata," objected Akudri, "I would like very much to stay here with the Mondeli. He has asked me to help him with his work, and he will teach me how to read and write Bangala. May I stay, Tata?"

Tata was not too happy with this arrangement, but Akudri was getting to be a young man. It must be at least fifteen dry seasons since he began to breathe his own air in his father, Dada's village. Too, it would be a real advantage to have a son who could read and write.

"Very well, my son, you may stay. But you be careful, and don't believe everything these white people tell you. Their stories are wierd, and we will invoke the wrath of the spirits by becoming involved with them." "Don't do anything that would cause the spirits to send another epidemic of walking sickness."

Thus Akudri stayed with the Bells, and became the Bwana's right-hand man. He helped him build a bigger hut by digging little holes to set upright poles in a large symmetrical square. Elephant grass was bound in bunches around the poles, making lathe into which they plastered mud. They cut yards and yards of bark string with which they tied larger poles for the roof structure to the walls, and tied heavy layers of grass for the roof. Later the walls and floors were plastered with sand and cow manure. The Africans were impressed with the size and beauty of this house. It was one like they would build for the chief to live in. "But", they concluded, "these white people were just as important as the chief".

They still wondered where these strangers came from. Had they dropped from the rim of the moon? Or did some roaring whirlwind spew them out into this area? Or had they come from the spirit world hidden under the depths of the Nzoro river? These questions remained unanswered, but life was very interesting with them.

The new hut remained unoccupied, and the Kakwas wondered why. After some days the tangba (drums) announced another safari, Bwana Bell had expected another missionary couple, but knew nothing of their plans so he said nothing. They were welcomed by shouts and dancing to the drums. This new man was quite short, "Like the tribes of the forest" thought the tall race of the Kakwas. They were introduced as Bwana and Madame Davis, and installed into the luxury of the brand new hut, still smelling of fresh cow manure. ❖

1955 - Steve, Pete & Edythe's son, celebrates his
2nd birthday in Adi, Zaire

Edythe buying bananas in Bunia, Zaire

Rev. Peter Brashler in his Everett home surrounded by memorabilia from his years in Africa.
*Photo by the Everett Herald*

## New Horizons
## Chapter 4

Jim Bell was a visionary man of many new horizons. He was born in Georgia to a southern aristocratic family. After his education he began a career in banking and from the very start he gave it his best. He dressed like a southern gentleman, and he acted like one. He worked as though the whole banking establishment was his responsibility. He became a slave to the work ethic, and very early in his career began to push out for new horizons of success. He would be a bank president at forty.

God abruptly changed all of that. Jim was a consecrated Christian, and dedicated to world missions. A missionary speaker from Africa came to his church and fired Jim with enthusiasm for reaching the lost in Africa. He decided to support the missionary project with a whole tithe of his impressive salary, and this in addition to the tithe he was already giving to his church. He would be recklessly generous with the Lord, and he would be one of God's financiers.

But God did not give him the satisfaction and peace of heart that he expected. He seemed to indicate to Jim that he wanted not only his money, but that He wanted Jim. He seemed to hear God saying, "Jim, I want you to get off your banking binge, and to get your gentlemanly anatomy to Africa. Right now you are riding a high horse, but I have a work for you to do amongst a lowly race of people. Now just a miserable minute!" argued the banker with God, "what are you suggesting? You need me in that bank to help finance your great work. This is ridiculous - sending me to Africa."

"O.K.," mused his Maker, "It's up to you. I'll not compel you to go. But that is my plan for your life."

It took Jim several weeks to capitulate. After much panting in prayer, he quit his job and found his way to Moody Bible Institute in Chicago. He arrived in his pearl-gray suit and Florsheim shoes. Very impressive.

He went straight to Dr. James Gray's office and presented

himself to the president. He pointed out his sacrifices in leaving his banking career in order to come here and prepare for the Mission field.

"Very well," responded Dr. Gray, "We are happy to have you here at Moody. You will share a room with another student. At the end of the hall you will find a mop bucket and a scrub brush, and a pair of overalls. Your first job will be to mop the bathroom, and scrub all of the toilets. Thank you very much for coming to Moody. May God bless you. Good day."

Jim certainly did not hear correctly! Surely, that godly old president would not expect Jim to scrub toilets! Why, they had servants for those jobs in his home. There's got to be a mistake. And overalls! What would his fellow bankers think of him now!

He found his way to his assigned room. It was more like a prison cell than a bedroom. He sat on the bed. It felt like an instrument of torture. He couldn't possibly sleep on this. He was miserable. And angry. He would catch the first train back to Atlanta and head straight for his bank. He would explain to his manager that this was all a big mistake. He would ask for his job again.

But Jim was not only a Christian; he was a spiritual one. He wouldn't think of going back without praying about it. He took out his New Testament and it fell open to Philippians chapter two. "Let this mind be in you which was also in Christ Jesus, Who being in the nature of God did not consider equality with God some thing to be grasped after, but made Himself of no reputation; and took upon Himself the form of a servant." And on he read about the Savior's wonderful example of being a servant.

The Holy Spirit drove that passage home like an arrow hitting a bull's eye. He wrestled in prayer. The banker finally emerged from his dingy room, clad in a pair of overalls, laden with a bucket, a mop and a scrub brush. In several hours the porcelain toilets were shining, and the floor was sparkling clean. The banker's face was drenched in common work-men's sweat, and looked a far cry from a bank executive in a pearl-gray suit. But his heart was as light as a bird. He had engaged in a deadly battle with the enemy, and the Holy Spirit had enabled him to win. He had left his fractured foe lying on the battle field, gasping for breath. Jim was on his way to the Mission field. The spiritual warfare lay ahead of him, but that initial battle was won. New horizons lay ahead for Jim on the Mission field. Many valuable lessons were learned during his several years at Moody.

Jim met a beautiful girl on the ship that sailed around the southern tip of Africa towards his destination up the east coast of Africa. Her name was Agnes Hurlburt, and she was the daughter of Dr. Charles Hurlburt, the General Director of the Africa Inland Mission. They were both headed for Mombasa, Kenya, and then by train and lake steamer on to the Belgian Congo. After about a year, Agnes' father performed the wedding ceremony.

One of their first assignments had been to open up the work in Kakwa land. They saw some very fine young men, amongst them Akudri, place their implicit trust in the Savior, and turn their backs on the pagan religion of the witch doctor.

Jim and Agnes stayed only a short time after the arrival of the Davises. Jim was a pioneer and he must push on to the new horizons of the pygmy forest. The Kakwas of course did not want to see them go. A number of both men and women had been wooed and won to Christ through Jim and Agnes. Why could they not stay along with the Davises, and the Africans would build a large compound for the missionaries? But God was pressing the Bells on to new horizons.

The Davises built on the foundation of the Bells. Their's became a ministry of building bridges across colossal cultural chasms. Great misunderstandings existed between the Kakwas and the whites. Why did the mondelis blow their noses into little white cloths, and then fold the contents into the little cloth and put in their pockets? Why did they want to save that stuff? What's more, why did they have pockets? Indeed, why did they have clothes? What was wrong with the nice soft pieces of goat or sheepskin that the Africans used as loincloths? Why did they wear those funny looking things on their feet? Why not use the little African sandals that they had carved out of the soft Konyuke wood. These were an invention of the Kakwas that were carved to fit the soles of their feet with a little platform for the heel, and another for the sole. There was a little peg at the front end where the Kakwas slipped their big toe on the one side, and their four other toes on the other. As they walked, the shoes would slap against the soles of their feet, and then on the ground, making a noise like "pakara-pakara"; "pakara" at each step. The name became a phonetic one, "pakara-pakara." But no, the white people had to wear what they called "tennis shoes." When they walked on these, the sound was altogether different than the pakara-pakaras. They sounded like "katara, katara, katara," as the rubber soles slapped on the ground. Hence, the tennis shoes were dubbed as "Kataras". In the Bangala vocabularies one still finds the word "Katara", meaning "shoe".

There were further cultural differences that were often offensive to the Africans. Why would the white man dare to step on another's shadow? Didn't they realized that a person's shadow was the departed spirit of some brother? How would they like to be trodden under by some thoughtless foreigner? Too, why did they not periodically kill a rooster, or a goat to offer as a sacrifice to the spirit world? Did they not realize that their careless neglect of these customs could cause another great catastrophe like the walking sickness?

Patiently and carefully the Davises studied the cultural patterns of the black people. Not with the intention of trying to destroy, or change the culture of these people, but only to "destroy that within their culture which would destroy them". The Davises believed that the Gospel was supracultural, and that Christianity was neither a white man's nor a black man's religion. They had no intentions of trying to change cultural patterns as long as they were not contrary to the teachings of the Bible, nor harmful to their bodies.

Customs such as bleeding a person's body to allow the spirit of sickness to escape; or drowning the second child of each pair of twins; or circumcision of girls as practiced in their cruel native ways; or knocking out several incisors out of the mouth of an adolescent girl in order to insure fertility were all customs that were very harmful to their bodies. The Davises taught them that all such manners were contrary to the teachings of Nzambe, and that there was a better way.

They also taught the basics of the Gospel. A number of those first converts were destined to become leaders of the future Adi Church. Among the very first ones was Akudri. He had often wondered about the superstitious beliefs and practices of the Kakwa tribe. He was very much afraid of evil spirits, but he had grave doubts as to the powers and practices of the witch doctor. He felt surely that this "Nganga na Bashenzi" was a phony. Ralph Davis taught about Yesu Kristu, that He was the true Son of Nzambe. That He had miracle-working power over all the demons. He read the scriptural account of the man who brought his demoniac son to the Master, having been tormented by this wicked spirit since childhood.

"If you are able to believe," read Davis, quoting the Master's words in Mark Chapter 9, "All things are possible to him that believes".

Akudri was engrossed with the story. "Do you mean that this Yesu Kristu has power to chase away the evil spirits? Does He also have power over sickness and death? Why, these demons are the terror of our tribe every day of our lives. We use up most of our wealth to provide sacrifices to appease the spirits. Is it true, we will no longer have to fear them if we become followers of Yesu Kristu?"

"That's exactly what I mean, Akudri." replied the missionary. "And furthermore, you won't have to fear death anymore. When your time to die comes, Yesu will be right there to take you to Lora, the place we call heaven."

From there Davis introduced the 23rd Psalm to them. The beautiful imagery of the sheep and the shepherd was not at all strange to the Kakwas. Akudri had known so well the responsibility of caring for sheep as he had for years provided food and water and security and rest for his father's sheep.

"No matter if I walk through the "mbudu" (valley) of the shaded area of death, I will fear no evil (not even the demons themselves)," interpolated Ralph Davis.

Akudri and four others were among the very first believers. They rejoiced in their new-found liberation from the terror of the spirits. Not that they would be free from the temptation and harassment of the spirits; but through prayer and further teaching, they were no longer under bondage.

Ellen Davis began to teach them the alphabet, and the fundamentals of phonemics. With the help of flash cards, she taught them the vowels; and finally the vowels joined to certain consonants such as BA-BE-BI-BO-BU, etc. Akudri was an apt pupil, and soon was able to write with his fingers in the dust all the letters of the alphabet, and also join them in combinations with certain consonants. He was also able to read certain verses that had been translated into Bangala.

Akudri likewise showed signs of real spiritual growth. He learned how to pray both privately and publicly. He was not ashamed to raise his resonant voice in prayer on behalf of his own personal needs, and also those of his family, and finally for all the Kakwa tribe. He was a man of prayer, and people heard him all over the village when he prayed. He had developed a good pair of lungs in his earlier years as leader of the village dances. As he prayed daily, the man of prayer also began to learn more and more about prayer. His burden for his immediate family was great.

One day some of his cousin/brothers arrived at Kukalunga. He saw immediately that they came with mawa (sorrow), because they wore mud and ashes on their bodies. They were filthy, and their hair was dishevelled. The eldest of the cousin/brothers had died. Tata had already called the witch doctor, and back in their village they were making sacrifices, and having their all-night orgies of drinking and wailing to appease the angry spirits. Akudri must come home to join in the procedures.

There was no way out for Akudri. He must go to his family in their grief and minister to them. The Davises had prayer with Akudri and his brothers before they left, praying especially for Akudri. It was certain that he would have a confrontation with the witch doctor, and also with certain pagan relatives who would also be hostile. Akudri felt fortified by the prayer, and went as a modern David to face his Goliath.

When he arrived with his brothers, the whole village was in a frenzy. Bodies filthy with mud and ashes, and blood flowing from the long lacerations they had cut deeply into their bodies. The flowing sweat and blood mingled together to cover their bodies with a mixture of filth. Many of them threw their tortured bodies on top of the dead body that lay beside the open grave. They made the weirdest noises and contortions as they danced round and round to chase away the evil spirits.

The scene was all too familiar to Akudri, and it sickened him. This had been his type of life until a few months ago. He was stricken with grief at the loss of a brother, but even more so because his family were still so engrossed in such wicked heathenism. When Kitoko, the beautiful young wife Tata had taken so recently, saw Akudri, she cried, "Oh Akudri, you have come. Now you can lead us in our dance of sorrow."

Her husband, Tata, agreed, "Yes, Akudri, my son, you are now my eldest son. You must take your place as the leader of the dance. This is what we trained you to be."

Akudri was perplexed. How could he, a Christian, indwelt by the Holy Spirit participate in these pernicious practices. On the other hand, how could he hurt his grief-stricken parents whom he had not seen in almost a year. Certainly, God would not want him to hurt them. Perhaps, after he had participated with them on this one occasion, he could persuade them too to accept Christ. What was he to do. Hurt his family, or hurt the missionaries, and even more seriously, hurt his new found Master?

As he pondered, he prayed. As he prayed he was reminded of Bwana Davis' prayer for him, that he would in no way bring shame on Nzambe, His Lord. He faltered between two opinions, but not for long. The recollection of Davis' prayer helped him to realize that this was no option. He had but one choice, and that was to stand firm with his family and declare his purpose to follow Nzambe's path.

"My dear brothers and sisters," began Akudri, "my heart

cries even more for all of you. I know the fear and the sorrow that you are going through. You fear because of this Nganga na Bashenzi," pointing to the witch doctor, "and the power that you think he has to either stay or start the wickedness of the demons. He has deluded you with many lies. I too have believed all my life as you do, but I have now come to know Yesu Kristu. He alone has power over the evil spirits, and over sickness and death. I can no longer participate in these pagan practices. I will have nothing to do with the dance, nor will I drink your masanga (beer). I have come to show you a better path, the path of Yesu Kristu," Akudri had spoken in a clear loud voice, and with great eloquence. The kind of eloquence that would make him famous as one of Africa's greatest preachers.

"Woe, Woe, Woe-ooah, - Woe, Woe, Woe-ooah!" screamed the witchdoctor as he began to froth at the mouth. "Akudri is possessed with the worst of demons! He must die immediately or the spirits will send another epidemic of the sickness that walks. The whole village will die! Akudri is a prince of devils! Kill this wicked devil!"

The Nganga started after Akudri with a razor-sharp knife, and would have killed him forth-with. But lo!, the witch doctor fell into a frenzied convulsion. Were it not for the fact that a higher Power, indeed, a Supreme Power was in control, this young stalwart soldier of Jesus Christ would have been cut short. Akudri was ordained of God, and all the principalities and powers of hell could not lift a hand against God's anointed. He was immortal in God's hand until he should complete the mission that God had for him. This was proven to Akudri that very moment, and such miraculous deliverances from death were to occur repeatedly during the course of his lifetime. The devil was thwarted in his plan to liquidate Akudri in Tata's village long ago, and he continues on, now in his mid-eighties, to literally laugh at his final foe, death.

Tata was pleased that his powerful son did not become a victim of the Nganga. Even if he would not cooperate in pagan practices, he could still be the head of the family. He could still be the leader of the dance celebrations of joy where the witch doctor would not be involved.

"Akudri, my son," said the father, "I want you to come back home to live. I need you to be the head man of my clan. I am old, and will soon be blown away by the spirits. You must take care of my gardens, and all of my flocks."

Kitoko was on hand too. She had made real advances in the affections of old Tata. Instead of being his third wife now, and a servant to the first two conniving cronies, she had become Tata's favorite wife. He had built her a beautiful new hut right next to his own. Kitoko was young and graceful. At the more and more infrequent times when Tata felt the urge to sleep with one of his wives, it was always Kitoko.

She joined with her husband in his plea to Akudri to come back home. Should old Tata die, this favorite son would fall heir to this young attractive wife, and Kitoko had been thinking much along those lines. The thought of this development crossed Akudri's mind occasionally since he had been home these few days, and that prospect looked rather alluring. The brothers too invited Akudri to come and take charge of the village. They offered him many enticements, even to the point of sending him to Uganda, the land just across the border, to search for greater riches for the clan. This was a tempting enticement to Yoane. The whole prospect looked very attractive to the young Christian, but he decided to first go back to Kukalunga to talk it over with Ralph and Ellen Davis.

He made the journey back to the missionary compound, and Bwana Davis had big news for him. Something that would prevent his immediate return to his family, and actually to cut ties with old Tata for good. He was never to see him again.

Not many months after Akudri had visited his village, Tata became ill and soon after he died. He had very much admired his son, Akudri, and was even intrigued with the news of Yesu Kristu. But he was still afraid of the witch doctor, and the evil spirit world. Akudri had witnessed faithfully to his father, but the old man never came to a place of trusting the Savior. This broke Akudri's heart. One by one all of the members of old Dada's family, and also those of his younger brother, Tata, accepted the Lord through Akudri's guidance, and he was able to baptize them.

The big news that Bwana Davis had for Akudri was that the sight of the Kukalunga Mission Compound was going to be moved to a place across the Nzoro River, and that after the move was accomplished, the Davises were going to be moved to the Zande tribe, some 400 miles to the north, to start a new work there. This big apple-cart upset of plans was to play a very important role in Akudri's life.

But Akudri shared with Ralph and Ellen that his family were counting on Akudri to come back home to head up the clan. This bit of news was very disturbing to the Davises because the young Kakwa convert showed real leadership potential, and they were praying about Akudri going with them to Zande Land. The three of them went to a sacred trysting place to meet with God in prayer. After hours of heart-searching, Akudri turned his back on his own country, and from his kindred, and his father's house, unto a land that was to be shown him by his Heavenly Father. He obeyed, and he went out, not knowing where he went.

Had he known then the physical suffering, the spiritual battles, the anguish of soul and the encounters with death that would lurk his path every step of the way, he might well have faltered.

"He went out, not knowing where he went." Heb. 11:8. ❖

Tadayo and wife, Perepetya

Mother & child of the Kakwa Tribe

Ken & Dorothy Richardson

## He went out to conquer new horizons
## Under the Shade of the Konyuke
## Chapter 5

It was decreed at Mission Headquarters, about 90 miles to the north at a place called Aba, that the Davises should go to Bafuka's village. Bafuka was the big chief in a Zande village that bore his name. However, before the Davises were to go they must find a new location for the mission work among the Kakwas. Kukalunga was too inaccessible, due to the Obi River, only about one mile to the west. "OBI" was the name given to this great river of the spirits by the Kakwa tribe, but it also flowed through many other tribal areas toward the Great River called the Zaire River. The Belgian colonialists solved that name problem by arbitrarily calling it the Nzoro River.

The Nzoro flooded into raging torrents through the rainy season, cutting off Kukalunga from the Government post and the outside world. It was decided that an area several miles west of the Nzoro would be desirable. The Davises, along with Akudri and several other Kakwa believers explored the area and found the place called the Adi Rock. It was about a mile beyond the river from Kukalunga, and considerably higher. There was a large granite hillock protruding out of the loamy soil, covering an area of several acres. At the edge of the Rock lived a subchief, Kapita Mite.

Even though Mite's village was only several miles from Kukalunga, the Kakwas living near the Adi Rock were of a different clan. The two villages, separated by the Nzoro, had almost no dealings with each other. Kapita Mite was not a little surprised to see a white man and white woman, along with the "ngambo"-Kakwas (across-the-riverites) exploring around Adi Rock. Did they not realize that this Rock was sacred? That it was the home of the much-feared Spirit of the Rain? That if they desecrated the Rock, that the Spirit of Rain would withhold rain from all of the area? These strangers needed careful watching, and Mite alerted his whole clan. All of the men must be ready with their spears.

If they were going to offend the Rain Spirit, then war would be declared, and these strangers killed.

Akudri was aware of the sacredness of the Rock, and he cautioned the Davises, "Asinziri malamu", he warned, explaining the whole situation to the explorers. "This large mound of granite, which looks like the back of a huge hippo emerging out of a river is easily desecrated, according to the traditions of the Kakwas," continued Akudri, "Whenever the rains become scarce, the Nganga na Bashenzi will kill a sheep, or a young bullock. The blood will be scattered in various places on the Rock. The meat of the whole carcass, sopo (offal) and all will be roasted for a feast. The women will brew large quantities of masanga, and liquor will flow in abundance. They will dance all night, and all of the next day. They will thus make the Rogue of the Rain happy again, and send the rain. If the rain doesn't come, they will lacerate their bodies, causing their own blood to flow. This Spirit of the rain is not to be trifled with." Akudri was very intense as he explained the situation and very graphically gesticulated the story to the Davises. "Zambi na Oyo" (Therefore), he continued, "Asinziri malamu (be very careful), not to break any of the bushes or trees, not to spit on the Rock, or urinate on it. Not to speak unkindly or disparagingly of it, because Mite and his men will be watching us through the eyes of a owl. They will shoot arrows in our bodies until they will look like the bulrushes sticking out of the marshes by the river."

They walked carefully across the Rock and discovered a Konyuke tree growing near the edge of the Rock. Under the shade of the scraggly tree, with its bony branches and broad leaves, they sat and rested. They talked about the Kakwas under the spell of witchcraft. They had a time of prayer, calling upon the Elohim of the Old Testament, who, as Ralph Davis explained, is indeed the Giver of the rain.

He read Genesis 7:4, "I will cause it to rain upon the earth". Also Leviticus 26:4, "I will give you rain in due season."

They implored God to open the eyes of Mite's people, and indeed, all of the Kakwas. Not only that they might know Him as the true Rain Giver, but also as the Giver of every good and perfect gift, even that of His own Son. Earnestly each one prayed that God would open this stronghold of Satan to the Gospel, that there might be a strong vigorous church in this area. How little did they realize that some 17 years later, when the author of this book and his wife were assigned to Adi, that they, with Yoane Akudri, would lead a host of several thousand Kakwa believers to the crown of the Rock of the Rogue of the Rain for an Easter sunrise service. Before the rising of the sun on that Easter Sunday of 1941, there would be a heavenly chorus singing triumphantly, "Christ the Lord is Risen Today, Hallelujah!"

By that time the Rain Spirit had really dried up and blown away. The Holy Spirit was in control, with the words of Jesus: "If any man thirst, let him come unto ME and drink. He that believeth on ME, as the Scripture says, out of his vitals shall flow rivers of living water." John 7:38.

After praying under the Konyuke, Davis and his party made tea and sat under that tree to refresh themselves. And to dream about the future. Just across the little valley, further to the west, was another rising plateau of fertile soil. That would make an ideal sight for a mission station for the Kakwa work. It would be called the Adi Station, not in honor of the Rogue of the Rain, but rather in honor of the "Rock of Ages", out of whose cleft side poured the Water of Life. Visions of a Chapel, a dispensary, a school building, and several missionary residences all flashed before their vision. God would do great things for them.

Thus dreaming under the Konyuke tree, their attention was drawn to the trunk of the tree. All around was granite, and vegetation was impossible. But here, incredibly, coming out of the granite stood a live tree with sap in its roots and trunk, and branches and foliage. How could such a miracle be?

They noted a tiny crack running through the granite. Some years before a bird must have carried a piece of acidulated fruit from another tree to the spot of the rift, there to enjoy its meal. One of the tiny seeds must have lodged in the small crack, found enough moisture and shelter under the moss to sprout a root. Down, down bored the hair-like root until it reached the loamy soil beneath the granite. The seed took strength and forced growth through the crevice to form a strong root. This produced a tiny seedling which continued to take nourishment from the soil underneath. It became a shelter for the birds, and in the rainy season, it produced a tart fruit, not unlike a crabapple. The branches produced a soft wood that would later, after the fear of the Rain Rogue was gone, provide the right kind of material from which they could carve spoons, ladles, sandals, and evenlong-pronged combs for their kinky hair. The fruit was tasty to the Kakwas, and they ate it in abundance during the rainy season. Another incidental blessing was that it served as the annual purge that God knew these manioc-munchers would need.

That Konyuke still stands as a landmark today of how God began to work at Adi station more than sixty years after Akudri and the Davises made it a place of prayer. It was a thrill for the author and his wife to stand under that tree just a short time ago. We were there for the purpose of researching this book, and to talk with Yisaya Wuli and Yeremiah Banga and other leaders. We recalled the seeds of prayers that have been dropped into the crevices of the granite hearts of many Kakwas and have produced countless "spiritual" Konyukes all through Kakwa land.

The little safari from Kukalunga to Adi Rock was only a five mile round trip, but it had been a long, worth-while day of praying and pondering and planning. Before returning they walked over to see the head man of the village, Kapita Mite to greet him, and to show him kindness. Mite was delighted to welcome these strange white people into his village. He too rather wondered if they had not fallen from the rim of the sliver of the new moon. He was relieved to hear Bwana Davis speak in Bangala as Davis and Akudri explained why they had come, and that they would be very careful not to desecrate the Rock. Mite was pleased, and assured the visitors that he would be very open to a Mission station nearby. They trekked back to Kukalunga, weary, but wondrously happy for what God had shown them under the Konyuke tree.

Akudri's next trek was a quick visit back to his home village. His family were all happy to see their brother and son, and to welcome him home as the king of the dance. But Akudri told them how God was leading him to go to the north to help Bwana and Madame Davis in their coming safari to the Zande tribe. Kitoko and all the family were distressed to hear this news. They did not want their favorite brother, the king of the dance, and the coming headman of their village to go away. He would most surely be torn limb from limb by some ferocious animal. He might possibly encounter some head hunters who would eat his flesh, and grind his finger and toe nails to a pulp so that this side dish could be ingested, and from which could be assimilated the spirit value of their prey. "Oh, Akudri", cried Kitoko to her stepson, "you must change your mind. If you don't we shall never see you again. If you want to help the missionaries in telling others about Yesu Kristu, you can do it right here among the Kakwas. We need you here near our own village."

"But, Kitoko," replied her stepson, "Bwana has asked me to go along to help him direct the porters and make them walk well. They have much equipment, and it will take 35 men to carry the loads. They will only go a few days journey, and then return home. We shall have to get a new team of carriers every two or three days to the next change point. Bwana does not know how to talk to the black people like I do. He needs me."

Indeed, Akudri knew how to talk to the black people. His clear clarion voice could sound ferocious when he turned up the sound decibels. He could shout down the most recalcitrant of rebels. Should they lay down their burdens and go on a strike, Akudri's voice would rear out like a lion and scare them out of their loincloths. His was the "voice of one crying out loud and clear in the wilderness." No wonder he was later called "Yoane" or "John", for he, like the first Baptist bearing that name, could certainly "prepare the way of the Lord, and make straight His paths".

Akudri bade his family farewell amidst strong crying and tears. He went back to Kukalunga and immediately began to help the Davises get their safari in order. It took several days of packing and repacking, and arranging individual packs into not more than 35 pounds each. There was much excitement in the compound, mingled with sadness. The Kakwas had learned to love these strange white people, even though their life style was so mysterious. By this time there was a growing group of believers, and they readily accepted Akudri as their leader, even though he was of a different clan.

When all was ready very early in the morning, at the first crowing of the first koko (rooster), the whole company gathered under a tree for a farewell service. Ralph preached in Bangala, and Akudri interpreted into Kakwa. Ellen Davis had translated some of the old hymns from an English hymnal into Bangala. These they sang with the greatest of enthusiasm to the beat of drums, but with a minimum of harmony. They loved to sing these new songs, but pity the musician with perfect pitch who was exposed to it. They sang and they prayed for those who were going on the long journey.

Then breakfast. There was an abundance of fufu (manioc mush), koko (boiled chicken), and gpedi gpedi (cooked greens mixed with lots of home ground peanut butter), and there was sufu (chicken gravy). The food was fabulous, and in abundance. The 35 Kakwas who would go as porters, the Davises, Akudri and the village Kapita were guests of honor, seated in a large circle on small kitipalas (small foot stools). All the rest of the group were seated in circles of about 20 in each, flat on the ground. In the center of each circle was a huge earthen pot of fufu. Smaller pots of boiled chicken, and still more pots for all the other goodies were added. All in order and Akudri prayed a thanksgiving prayer for the food . Not too long a prayer, as he no doubt was as hungry as the rest of them. "Amen" was pronounced, and immediately began the steady noise as of a rushing stream. Not a voice was heard, as this was serious business. Feasting was important. Chops were licked, and tongues were clicked, and hiccups were hicked. The noise of the rushing stream arose into a crescendo. For about 25 minutes not a word was spoken, not even a "please pass the chicken." It would be much more polite to reach past the one next to you than to disturb him with a request for food. Volumes of victuals were voraciously vanquished before the hungry bellies were satisfied. Then began the burps. It would be a insult to the hostess not to burp, for it was through a bellowing burp that one expressed his delight in the meal. The louder the burp, the more pleased was the hostess.

The Davises were amused as well as amazed with such a gourmand's delight. Actually, they did not have a connoisseur's palate for such a meal. They ate sparingly, to the dismay of the hostess, because they did not want to take a chance on purupuru. This is that embarrassing sickness of the sopo (stomach) that often accompanies such an extravagant gastronomic experience. But they very much enjoyed the fellowship. Now they were ready for the safari.

The 35 porters lined up for their head packs, and some of the villagers hoisted the loads and set them squarely on the heads of the safari crew. Straight of back, with burdens balanced symmetrically on their heads, these beasts of burden were ready for their task. The tepoy was set up for Ellen, consisting of two long parallel palm poles with a seat woven of elephant grass secured between the poles with bark string. A little foot rest was tied on the seat to serve as a foot support for Ellen's feet.

The missionaries were ready with their pith helmets set squarely on the tops of their heads. The Kakwas were always amused at these white round hats with a little veranda fastened all the way around them. This pith helmet would for many years serve as the status symbol for the strange white people. The Davises were also adorned with new pairs of white Kataras (tennis shoes) and Ralph wore a pair of khaki shorts, and a khaki bush jacket, while Ellen wore a long khaki skirt.

All was set, but they would not think of starting such a journey without first committing themselves to Nzambe's care. Ralph produced a small pocket testament, and as he read from the English he translated into Bangala. "I will lift up my eyes to the hills, from where does my help come? My help comes from Nzambe (Elohim). He who keeps you will not fall asleep. Nzambe holds you tight in His strong hands. Nzambe is your shade so the sun cannot burn you in the day time, and the moon will not frighten you in the night. Nazambe will guide your departure, and will cause you to return safely again. He will walk before you on the path of life for days and days without ever finishing. Amena!"

With the Psalm read and appropriated by all of them, it became their safari Psalm for the whole journey with preparations all made, Ellen, like an oriental queen, mounted her throne in the tepoy, and was carried by four stalwart blacks. This was the throne she would occupy for the whole month. Ralph had to walk, and he would develop more than a few blisters on the long journey ahead.

The 35 porters followed in the procession. The villagers too, in a large company, followed them to the Nzoro River. Being dry season, the travellers crossed the river without a problem. This was the separation point. Basenenes (farewell greetings) were quiet and subdued, bathed with much mai-misu (water of the eyes). When would they ever see their Kakwa brothers again? What about this lovable, laughing, lavishing little mondeli, whom many of the Kakwas called Bwana "Dabisi"? Most of them used v's and b's interchangeably, hence, Bwana "Davis" became Bwana "Dabisi". They would never, unless as in later years, some fussy school teacher would try to change them, think of ending a word with a consonant. So they simply added the "i" to the Dabis. No, they would never find another Bwana Dabisi. Nor would they find such a queenly little woman as Ellen Davis. Yes, their hearts died with sorrow.

The whole trip was quite uneventful, though extremely interesting for the whole party. They went through wild animal country where they saw huge herds of buffalo. There were hundreds of water buck, and many other species of antelope. Elephants and even prides of predatory lions, as well as wart hogs, hyenas, wild dogs, and all kinds of primates, including baboons, and chimpanzees and many species of monkeys. This made Ellen a bit apprehensive, but Akudri reassured her. In the first place, the pilgrims Psalm (#121) that Bwana Dabisi had read was still very much in vogue. Furthermore, the Kakwas were great hunters, and they knew the habits of the animals. They would be careful not to frighten the larger and dangerous animals.

But the Kakwa porters would not think of going through such a game paradise without remembering their perennially pleading sopos (stomachs). Many of the lovely gdobies (bush buck) were bagged with their bows and arrows, and taken along for the evening meal. They were uncanny in their expertise as archers, and could pierce a guinea fowl through the heart at 75 yards. Several of these large birds would make a meal for the whole group.

The 35 porters stayed with them for several weeks before deciding to return to their families in Kakwa land. From there on they had to engage local carriers each morning who would serve them only for a day. God blessed them with good carriers. Only a few of them tried to play a trick on this white man by laying down their burdens in the middle of the day and refusing to go further unless their pay would be doubled. In such instances Akudri proved to be an effective arbitrator. He took no nonsense from striking porters. His heart was big enough to give his loin cloth to one in need, but he had a special aversion to anyone who would try to cheat his Bwana. He could shout at them like a longshoreman foreman. He created the impression that he was capable of thrashing them to within an inch of their life. Yet he never laid a hand on one of them, and he was always fair. After talking some sense into them he would witness to them about Christ. By that time, the offender was usually so scared that he would gladly make a commitment, simply in order to get this Kakwa off his back. Each day, after the porters had done their work, they prepared a good meal for them, gave them a portion of salt, and a square of soap, and then a few francs. Nor would Akudri let them go without making the Gospel very clear to them, and a number of them confessed the Lord Jesus.

It took about six weeks before they reached Bafuka, having passed through Aba, the Mission's Headquarters station, where they rested about 4 days. Their next stopping place was Dunqu, the first station in Zande land. They finally reached Bafuka, the end of their journey. They had travelled something over 400 miles. Ellen was glad to surrender her throne, and her royal carriage for the luxury of a mission station. There she was given a hot bath, and for the first time in many weeks she could stretch out in a full sized bed, sharing it with her husband.

Akudri stayed with the Davises for about six months, and his help in getting this work started was invaluable. However, Akudri was burdened for his own tribe, the Kakwas. He prayed earnestly for his people, and shared his burden with Ralph and Ellen. Davis read for Akudri Rom. 9:1-3: "I have great heaviness and continual sorrow in my heart. For I could wish that I myself could be accursed from Christ for the sake of my brethren, my kinsmen according to the flesh."

The Spirit used these verses and Akudri could say with Paul, "My heart's desire and prayer to God for the Kakwas is that they may be saved".

The Director of the Mission, Bwana Hurlburt told Davis to go back to Aru in order to get official permission from the government to start a mission station at Adi. Akudri and Davis made that safari all the way back to Aru, only 50 miles from Akudri's home and Adi. At Aru they made proper arrangements with the Territorial Administrator for papers for a concession of land, and official permission to occupy the plateau at Adi. Davis left Akudri there to go on back to Adi by himself, while he, Davis, went back to Bafuka. He was much disappointed to lose Akudri, but he gave him a letter of recommendation. ❖

1954 - Pete with Edythe and their son, Steve,
(age 11 months) enroute to Africa.

## Special People
## Chapter 6

Kenneth Richardson had finished his tour as a soldier in the British Army. He had learned not only to live under discipline, but also to discipline. Upon his discharge he promptly married his sweetheart, Dorothy. They were young. They were romantic, and they had a zest for life. Most important, they were dedicated Christians with a deep desire to serve the Lord as missionaries, somewhere in Africa.

With the wedding rice shaken out of their clothing, their hair and their shoes, they presented themselves forthwith to the British Headquarters of the Africa Inland Mission in London. They went through the gruelling test that the A.I.M. was wont to give to missionary candidates, and created a good impression. There was no question about their conversion experience, their doctrine, their academic qualifications and their suitability. They gave a clear statement of their call to the Mission field, and were soon accepted as missionary candidates.

In the spring of 1924 they bade farewell to their families and friends. A Baptist Church in Highgate, London became their home and sending church. The farewell service was conducted with typical British reserve. There were no tears, nor anything emotional for this ex-soldier; and Dorothy had her image all carved out for her. To weep at a farewell service was a sign of weakness. Not even a hidden honk into one's handkerchief would be tolerated. They soon found themselves in a compartment of a British train, leaving Victoria Station for Southampton. Fortunately, they had the compartment to themselves, with their things scattered through the compartment. Once Dorothy began to feel the movement of the train, and the vibration of the rails, she began to realize what was happening. She was a tall, stately woman with typical British aplomb, and she was determined that she would be a match for her military man. She would not allow her husband to see any of her tears. But those waving loved ones at the train station were just too much. Pretty soon a big tear drop spilled over her cherubic cheek. Ken pretended not to see it. Handling a rookie soldier would have been like a British cup of tea for him, but a grown woman of aristo-cratic bearing, one who was his own wife, with tears in her eyes! "What on earth could he say to her?" he mused.

He looked out of the train window, feigning ignorance of the whole situation. Soon Dorothy's frame became convul-sive, like a little girl going off to boarding school for the first time. Actually, she was overcome with emotion like any other normal bride at the thought of leaving hearth and home for the first time. Furthermore, she was turning herself completely over to a man with whom she was not yet very well acquainted. Now she was under his control. What had she let herself in for?

But Ken arose to the occasion. With his Irish linen handkerchief he dabbed awkwardly at her eyes, and let her blow her patrician nostrils into it. "There, there, Dollie, it's okay. We are together, and God is going before us."

He had never called her "Dollie" before, but is sounded good to him. He would use that as his affectionate nickname for her. She liked the sound of it too, and she was pleased to hear him call her "Dollie". This became Ken's special nickname for her from then on.

Ken and Dollie had opportunity to really discover what kind of spouse each had taken. They were both delighted in the discovery. No more tears. Ken had been equal to the crisis, and the two hearts were inseparably entwined to-gether for a long romantic life together that would include a medley of joys and sorrows.

The train eventually arrived at Southampton, England's leading shipping port on its southern coast. The newlyweds were thrilled at the sight of the ocean liners. With the help of their passenger agent they found the ship which would be their honeymoon-home for the next several weeks, and carried on their baggage. Their freight for Africa was stowed in the hold of the ship. A few friends had driven down from London to bid them their final farewell.

With a blast of the whistle, and a call from the cockney

steward "All ashore what's goin' ashore," the ship was soon being nudged into the English channel. It was late in the afternoon when they set sail, and they did not expect to return for another five years. The thought of that caused a rather sinking feeling, and along with the churning of the channel, and the erratic behavior of the ship, the newlyweds were beginning to feel sick with a sickness that was definitely not love-sickness. They found their way into their cabin, and absolutely ignored the gonging of the dinner bell. "Sea sickness can be 'orrible," the cockney steward comforted them.

It took them several days to find their sea legs, and by that time they were sailing in the South Mediterranean Sea. The water was calm, and the weather balmy. This was more like a honeymoon. They had a heavenly voyage, and with ample time to bask in one another's presence, and to walk arm in arm over the rolling deck. They absorbed much sunshine and sea air. Going to the dining room was also a fun experience for them. No more sea sickness.

They had ample time to dream about the future, to study their Bibles together and to set goals for their marriage. Ken recorded in one of his later books:

> "To one of Africa's dark places my wife and I were directed in 1924. The Mission field looked so rosy, seen from England's shores. The voyage out took us through the Mediterranean, up the White Nile to Rejaf, thence by car across the border of the Belgian Congo (now Zaire), to Aba, the Headquarters of the Africa Inland Mission. We were filled with excitement."

(From "Pioneering Among the Kakwa" - K. Richardson)

This trip was all they could have wished for. Dolly discovered that her soldier husband was a serious student of the Bible. He would find a lonely spot on the ship, leaving his wife on a deck chair to write or read, while he searched the Scriptures. Then they would go to their cabin together to pray. During these trysting times, they covenanted together that they would ask God to give Ken the gift of communicating the Scriptures in a simple understandable way to the Africans, just like their sending pastor had advised. God marvelously answered that prayer by giving Ken unusual insight, and the gift of teaching in several African languages, as well as in English.

The trip to Africa ended all too soon, but not the honeymoon. They never seemed to get over the idea that their life together should be a continual honeymoon, with God right in the center of it. They sailed up stream on the Nile to Juba in the Sudan. This must certainly have been the hottest place on earth, thought the honeymooners. They made the trip by motor car (a la British) to Aba by Bwana Paul Hurlburt, the Field Director of the A.I.M. Congo field.

After about a week at Aba they made ready for their trip to Adi. Dollie was to be carried in a tepoy, carried by four coal-black huskies of the Logo tribe. They were big, with rippling muscles, and clad in the scantiest of loin cloths. Their big buttocks were just no match for those tiny and dirty shreds of cloth that they had stuffed under cowhide belts. Dollie sat stately in her chair, but when the four blacks stepped into place in front of her, and she had to actually face those glistening, bare black bottoms, it was absolutely shattering to Dollie's British sense of decency.

" Ken," she called out to her khaki-clad confidant, "You must do something about this horrible situation. I can't possibly ride behind such scenery!" Ken felt sorry for his Dollie, but he was at a loss to know what to do. "Don't worry, Dollie Dear," he stammered in what was left of his Oxford English accent, "I'll think of something."

Poor Ken pondered a good deal over the dilemma, but what he was going to "think" about did not materialize. Dollie had a large white serviette, which she pinned on the veranda around her pith helmet. "To keep the sun out of my eyes," she explained to Ken. But the veiled helmet really had a dual purpose; the main one of which was to keep the glowing glisten of the sweaty behinds out of her sight.

After several days in the bush the black bottoms seemed

to have lost their horror for Dollie, and there were many other things to occupy their attention. Like a true Trojan, she had met and passed another crisis. Her magnificent sense of humor did not desert her, and she finally saw the funny side of it. The two of them were able to laugh hilariously about it in the privacy of their side by side camp cots in the middle of the night. Someone has observed that for missionaries these are two essential qualities: 1) a good sense of humor, and 2) a poor sense of smell. They qualified well at least in the first one of these.

The trek to Adi took about five desiccating days. Late in the afternoon Dollie would ask one of the carriers who knew a bit of English, "How much farther before we stop for the night?"

"Kuna na ngambo (across that next stream)," the African would reply, sticking his tongue out in the direction of the distant ravine. They would brace themselves for the next mile or two, glad that the day would soon be over. Finally reaching the river, they crossed it and began the ascent on the other side. On and on they trekked on their bare feet, the Africans had no intention of stopping. Finally the dialogue would be repeated, and "Kuna na ngambo" was the same response. This was repeated for several more crossings before darkness would finally settle in to stop them. They were glad to reach the end of their long trek and finally arrive at Adi. The believers were very glad to welcome them, and to fill a huge earthen pot of water behind a little bush shelter where they could properly bathe themselves, even though it had to be in a standing position.

Wuli, Araba and Atandi, each of whom was destined to become a leading pastor of the Adi Church were on hand to receive the Richardsons, and to be their hosts. They had a nice mud and pole hut all fixed up, and the honeymooners were ready to settle in for a long career at Adi. Upon arrival, they were weary and a bit lonely. It would never do for these ascetic missionaries to admit this even to each other. Little did they realize at that time that Ken was destined of God to be used most significantly in the building up of the Adi Church, and that he would influence Akudri's life more than any other human being.

Soon after the Richardsons' arrival, Akudri made his appearance bearing official documents that Ralph Davis had procured at Aru. These included documentation for a free grant of 12 acres of land, bordering the Adi Rock upon which to build a Protestant Mission, including a chapel, a school for boys and one for girls, a dispensary and a residence for missionaries. Another letter that Akudri carried was his recommendation from Ralph Davis as a faithful and honest Christian worker.

Ken was favorably impressed with Akudri right from the start. He proceeded, however, with typical British caution in regards to letting him take on Pastoral duties. He must have a good grounding in the Word, and Ken must have ample time to disciple this young disciple. Akudri's first job with the Richardsons was that of chief cook. Every morning he was kept busy in the cook-house, and in the afternoons he visited the surrounding villages, beginning at Mite. He faithfully witnessed how God had enabled him to cheat his brother's grave during the epidemic of the sickness that walks, and how he had turned his back on the animistic religion of the Kakwas, and had accepted Yesu Kristu. His bold approach angered many of the older Kakwas, but many others, especially amongst the young men, were impressed. A few of them confessed Christ as their Savior. Akudri was not too sure about his new Bwana, after having to do with Jim Bell, a very "southern" American and extremely generous; one who unabashedly wept over the lost estate of the Kakwas. And then with "Dabisi", a very "American" American, very unreserved, quick to laugh, even a bit raucously at times, Akudri thought Richardson was "gudi pinza" (very different).

In the first place, who ever heard of a name like "Risisi". They never did learn how to properly pronounce "Richardson". The "ch" sound was foreign to them, so that became a simple "s". Then linking the "r" and the "d" and the "s" together was a combination absolutely unheard of. It was as bad as putting a Kakwa, a Lugnbara and a Logo all together in the same swamp to hunt one single buffalo. The result was chaotic. Akudri could come up with nothing better than "Risisi," and that continues to be the pronunciation to this day.

Dorothy took charge of Akudri in the kitchen. Yoane, like her new husband, learned from this matriarch to make a proper cup of tea. He also became very proficient in the fine culinary arts of British cookery. Even to this day he can cook up a meal of the most delectable delicacies that can entice the taste of the British and Americans alike.

Even in this menial milieu Akudri showed qualities of character and leadership. But the Richardsons kept a close watch on him. They never had reason to believe that he would "pinch" (Dollie's expression for stealing) any of her salt, sugar, soap or soup. They never once caught him telling a lie. This was evidence that he was born of the Spirit, because to the old tribes of Africa, stealing or lying was never a sin until it was proven in a person.

The mud hut that the Richardsons lived in was quite inadequate. Dollie dreamed of new brick home - a proper house as she put it. It would have beautifully white-washed walls and ceilings. It would have three bedrooms, a sitting room, a dining room, and a magazine (store room), and a study for Ken. Never mind a kitchen - that could be in the cook house outside. But a "must" was a small sewing room for Dollie, with a big window to let in lots of light. It would be properly covered with beautiful sawn timbers and woven elephant grass mats. Quite a dream, but Dollie was serious. Even Ken would concur with her, "yes, yes, Dollie, dear. We shall have a proper home." He was, however, a bit dubious about Dollie's dreams.

The first big task was to gather workmen and materials. God met that problem by sending Drupa, a long-limbed, gawky, ungainly, rather slow-witted young man, to the station. He was the newly appointed paramount chief of the Kakwas, and his old retiring father was with him. He, and his eldest son came to Adi to make an official call on the new missionaries. The old superannuated, slightly senile patriarchal chief was still in the "driver's seat", but Drupa, in his late teens was taking over the chieftainship.

Akudri made tea for the visitors as Dollie seated them the shade of a tree. Ken explained to the royal visitors his desire to launch a building program. "Our big problem", continued Ken, "is the matter of workmen. How can we get enough Kakwas to come and work for us?"

The Patriarch and the upstart had a few words in Kakwa. "Kulaazi te" (no affair), answered the chief in Bangala. "I will send fifty men who will work every day for one month. From them you can select one who will make a good Kapita (head man), and from the rest you can choose the best workmen to make up your regular crew. For the 50 days you can give each man a portion of salt, a square of soap, and a daily portion of posho (food ration)."

This sounded like an answer to Ken's prayers, and the beginning of the fulfillment of Dollie's dreams. "Oh, merci mingi (Oh, thank you very much)," exclaimed Ken to the chief. "That is very kind of you".

With several more cups of tea, lavishly laced with cream and sugar, and the consumption of a generous platter of biscuits (equivalent of sugar cookies), the royal visitors were on their way. This was the beginning of a long friendship between Akudri and the new young chief. Akudri showed Drupa the way of life on many occasions, and at one time he made a confession of faith. However, the chief was never ready to give up his masanghga (beer). He finally ended up a hopeless alcoholic, but he was always helpful to the church and the missionaries.

Ken's gang of 50 showed up, and they worked well for him as long as he stayed with them. As soon as he would leave, however, they would seek out the nearest shade and lie down for a sleep. Ken was anxious to find a Kapita amongst them. There were five that impressed him. After several days of watching, he eliminated #1 as prospective Kapita because he was abominably lazy. A day or two later he eliminated #2 because he was deplorably dumb. He just could not catch on. The third one was eliminated because he was an incessant liar. He could not be trusted. Number 4 was ruled out because Akudri had caught him in the act of stealing salt. If he would be Kapita he would have the whole crew stealing the missionary blind.

Ken was about ready to hire the fifth one even though he was a bit slow, when one morning he didn't show up. In the afternoon he staggered in, soused to his eyebrows. The most potent-smelling liquor that Ken had ever opened his nostrils to, reeked the whole place. Ken was thoroughly disgusted, and he let him sleep it off. The next day he sent him packing.

Still no Kapita, so Ken himself stayed through the long hours of hot sunshine to keep his gang working. But the sun was too much for Ken whose blood was already loaded with malaria parasites. He had to go to bed with a high fever. Akudri came to pray with him, and to discuss the work project.

"Bwana", suggested Akudri, "why don't you make that lazy one the Kapita? He may be lazy, but he has intelligence and leadership. Too, he has worked for the Belgians and he has many skills."

"Very well, Akudri," said the sick missionary who was chilled to the bone, and simultaneously exuding rivulets of rancid sweat from his quivering body, "You do what you think is right, and don't forget to pray for me."

Akudri left the sick room and gathered all the believers for a prayer meeting. Araba led off by praying earnestly for the Bwana. Then Atandi, another bright Christian, and Wuli, and Banga, and many others.

In the morning Dollie felt her lover's brow. The fever had broken. Ken still felt like a squeezed out sponge, and was as helplessly weak as an ant riddled post. But Dollie came in with a cup of her stimulating tea. He was confined to his bed for about a week, but he was on the mend. He had survived his first, and no doubt, the worst bout that he would ever have with malaria.

The lazy worker, appointed Kapita, came to Ken's bedside every morning. Ken would outline the day's work for him, and the volume he expected from the crew. It so happened that this Kapita who was too lazy to work well himself would not tolerate in the other workmen what he himself was guilty of, namely, laziness. He must have been from a chief's clan, because he knew how to lead, and to drive his men.

Beautiful bright red bricks were carried up from the kiln to the building site on the heads of women and teenaged girls, many thousands of them. Ken was able to be up and around again so he helped them lay the foundation bricks. With a good deal of trial and error the first courses of bricks were laid. Some of the workers had had experience with Belgian masons, and they became valuable workers to Ken. The end result was a beautiful colonial-style house, white-washed with what Africans call pembe, found in certain stream beds.

It was a great day for Ken and Dollie when they moved into their first home. Furniture had to be made, including a large bed-stead with a white muslin mattress sack which was filled with Kapok cotton from the Kapok trees that grew in the area. These beginnings were quite primitive, but the newlyweds were too much in love to take notice. They were extremely happy, and were fast making friends with the Kakwa people. People who so recently were paganized, and worshipped the spirits of their dead ancestors, under the control of Satan.

After Ken had been discharged from the British Army, having felt the call to go to Africa as a missionary, he was advised to take a course in dispensing medicines. He enjoyed that work very much, and seemed to have a real knack for treating diseases. The doctors of the Mission had equipped him with the basic instruments needed, and a good supply of medicines, which he was able to use in-treating many African diseases.

One of the first that came for treatment was a man with a serious case of malaria that had turned into Black Water fever. This was a kidney disease resulting from overdoses of quinine in the treatment of malaria. In the majority of cases for the Africans it was fatal, unless the right treatment was given.

Ken read all the medical books he had and found very little to help him treat this patient. He and Dollie and the church people prayed much, realizing how important to the work a cure of this man could be to their work. Ken took all quinine away from the sick man, and made him drink many liquids
The only last resort was prayer.

The patient survived the next few days, and miraculously

passed a crisis. God had intervened. Word spread like a grassfire in the dry-season wind. Bwana Risisi had cures that were better than those of the Nganga na Bashenzi. They began to come with sick babies. Ken examined them and then lifted his heart in despair to God. "Oh, God, if you don't help me, how can I heal these hopelessly sick people?"

God did help Ken affect many cures, and his reputation as a Monganga spread far and wide. The little "Pitaro" (African pronunciation for "hospital") became famous. It also became a real field for evangelism. He discovered, amongst the believers an intelligent young man named Yeka, who was capable of carrying out instructions. Yeka became Ken's "nurse" in the pitaro, and he was quick to learn. He took to medical work like a monkey to a stalk of bananas. After several years with Richardson, Yeka went to the Aba Hospital to take a course in paramedics under Dr. Kleinschmidt and his nurse/wife, Coralee. After completion of this on-the-job training with Dr. Kleinschmidt, Yeka became the "Monganga" of the Adi Pitaro. He had a very distinguished career as such for over 30 years. He was one of the long-standing elders of the church. ❖

David & Joyce Richardson
Joyce was the first white baby born among
the Kakwa Tribe.

Akudri with his wife, Maria, and family in Adi, Zaire

## What Praying Is All About
## Chapter 7

Two little black boys, beautifully adorned in their ebony skins, were hiding behind an ant hill. Covered with a loin cloth made of a strip of lingerie, which the Madame had left on the veranda as a dust cloth, these little urchins peered over the top of the knoll. They were careful not to reveal their presence to the Bwana, who himself thought he was hidden from view.

Ken had built himself a little grass shelter with a thatched roof over it to keep him sheltered from the sizzling sun, or from the staggering storms. He was totally unaware of the two pairs of spying eyes peeking through the crevices of the ant hill. The two little clandestine characters wanted to do a bit of research on this strange missionary from a strange country, and of strange behavior.

Richardson was indeed strange to the Kakwas. Every morning he left his beautiful mwasi (wife) alone in the big colonial house while he ventured off to his secret hiding place. He went to pray, and he wanted to be quiet and uninterrupted. The work of planting a church among the Kakwas was discouraging. Only a few were responding to the Gospel. Of those who did confess the Savior, far too many slipped back into pagan practices. Ken knew that the devil was opposing the work, and he felt that the only way to overcome was through prayer. This was his most effective weapon against his foe.

The kids on the station, however, thought that the white man was up to some hanky panky. What was he doing out there each morning by himself? They finally concluded that the new Bwana was in league with the devil. He must be in contact with evil spirits. The two little spies decided to find out what was going on. It was a dangerous mission, they thought, because they were intruding into the realm of evil spirits. They must be extremely quiet. Like a sleeping pair of crocodiles, camouflaged under the foliage of a tree, they lay as quietly as death. Under the guise, however, they were extremely alert. They were close enough both to see and to hear all that was going on.

Ken first opened his Bible and read for what seemed an interminable time to the spies. Then, falling on his knees, he began to groan. "Oh, Nzambe! Oh, my God; Oh, God the Father; Oh, God the Son; Oh, God the Holy Spirit". He was in the immediate presence of the Triune God. As he groaned, the tears began to roll. He had a picture of God, the Son on the Cross. This vision overwhelmed him as he languished in God's presence, reflecting the Cross and its meaning. He began to pray about the Kakwas. Here he saw a hell that was populated with pagan Kakwas. This was too much for him. He rolled over from his knees to a supine position, with his face toward heaven and arms reaching out to God. He was bathed in sweat as he wrestled with God on behalf of the Kakwa people. With strong crying and tears he poured out his heart before God.

The clandestine cronies behind the ant hill could not figure this out. Just what, in the Name of Nzambe, was going on? They did not realize that the Bwana was in a deadly fight with the old Jaboro (Diablo) himself. They lay quietly for about a half hour as the battle went on. Finally the urchins had enough. They were scared out of their loin clothes. As quietly as they had come, they crept away from their hiding place, and made their way back to the station. They gave a full report to the other kids. They decided this was indeed a case of a mortal man wrestling with the devil and they were terrified. They would have to report this to Akudri.

Akudri was not unfamiliar with Richardson's prayer antics, and he himself had begun the habit of praying much in the same manner. However, because of the report of the two spies, the next morning he hid himself behind the same ant hill. Ken's performance was much the same as it had been the day before. Akudri lay concealed, absolutely enraptured. He saw a man who was in God's presence, pleading for the Kakwa people. Even though he could not understand the English petitions, he could feel in his bones the sacredness of the hour. It was for him a lesson in prayer that he never forgot.

Akudri felt that this strange Bwana of his was a real man of prayer, and he wanted to emulate his example. He found a secret place of his own, and began a daily tryst of prayer much in the same manner as he had seen Richardson do from behind the ant hill. Even to this present day, 60 years later, to hear Akudri pray is indeed an unforgettable lesson in prayer. The way he says "Oh, Nzambe! - Nzambe na ngai (Oh God, my God)", makes one realize that his prayer is not merely a series of platitudes and cliches. He is really talking to God.

Some fifty years later, when Ken Richardson's body lay peacefully in a London cemetery, David Richardson, Ken's only son, took Akudri to see the grave. Yoane was very subdued as he thought of his old mentor. Kneeling on the grave, with tears streaming down his face, he prayed, "Oh, Nzambe! Nzambe na ngai." Other visitors stood aghast as they heard the black preacher from Zaire praying in this manner. To son, David, it brought heaven to earth because it was like hearing his own Dad praying once again.

Many of the black leaders in the church at Adi learned to pray in the same manner. Yakobo Ata would stand in the midst of the large congregation, with face toward heaven, praying as though he were talking face to face with God. His own face was aglow with the glory of God as he reflected this glory. In the next instant he would spill "mai-misu" (tears) all over his cheeks, and let them roll onto his shirt. He was praying for lost relatives.

Years later, when Edythe and I were assigned to Adi, we noticed Yakobo going past our home, reading a letter. We greeted him and asked him if he had received good news.

"Oh no," he replied, "this is not a waraga (letter), this is my 'liste' (prayer list), and it has 25 names of unsaved neighbors on it. I am praying for them. I pray for these every day, and I try to visit each one every week with the 'Sango Malamu na Yesu'"-(the Gospel of the Lord Jesus). Several months later I saw him again with the same piece of paper, very soiled, and almost all of the names, indicating that they had accepted the Savior. Adi indeed had become a place of prayer. One would never think of starting a journey, whether only a couple of miles by bicycle, or whether half way around the world for a furlough, without first having prayer. This secret was one of the richest legacies that Ken and Dorothy left the Adi Church.

Ken and Dollie had never gotten over the idea that they were lovers. Theirs was a honeymoon that endured until death "did them part". They were always very solicitous over each other. If Ken appeared to look rather weary, Dollie was sure he had malaria. "Oh Ken, you look ill", she would lament. "You must go to bed for a nap."

If Ken's bride appeared peaked then Ken would be the worried one, "Oh Dollie, darling, do you feel well? Let me fix you a cup of tea while you lie down and rest."

In spite of such solicitations, Dollie appeared at breakfast one morning looking as white as the manioc flour that covered the big flat rock near their home. "Oh, my word, Dollie, what on earth is wrong?" muttered the missionary.

"Oh Ken, I feel terrible. I've never had anything like this before." With that she streaked to the bathroom and grabbed a handy basin, just in time to avoid a nasty situation. Ken was frightened. He bathed her hot head, and put her to bed.

After several hours she felt better and got up. Everything seemed okay. It must have been something she had eaten. But the next morning there was a repeat performance after she had gotten out of bed. She was miserably sick and nauseated so she went back to bed again. After several hours she felt fine again. This kept up day after day and Ken was very alarmed. What was happening to his little Dollie? They would have to get word to the nearest doctor, but he was at least 85 miles from Adi. They prayed about the situation much, and worried not a little. They both were firm believers in prayer however, and they would just trust the Lord. Could it be cancer, was Ken's biggest worry. Or perhaps some virulent tropical disease.

Dollie began to be a little suspicious. How long had it been since she had had her last menstrual period? It seemed like an unusually long time. She'd wait yet for a week or two before suggesting anything to Ken. After all, she had heard that some women skip a month or more in such a tropical climate. But Ken was worried, and he prayed for a way to get a doctor.

One morning, after their devotions, Dollie decided to make her confession. But how to broach such a subject to a man? It had been bad enough in her younger days to talk to her mother about such subjects. She'd better wait a few days.

But Ken was very concerned. He wanted to send a bicycle messenger to Aba to see if he could get help. Dollie knew that she must share her secret. "Ken", she stammered, "I've got news for you". Then she burst into tears.

"Come, come, Dollie dear, whatever is the matter? Do you have a growth? Do you think it's a tumor? We shall pray that it will be benign!"

"Oh Ken, it's not that. I think we're going to have a baby." There, the secret was out. How would Ken ever forgive her?

"What was that?" stammered hubby - "did you say 'baby'?" Had it been 60 years later, and in an American culture, he would have said, "You've got to be kidding."

"Oh Dollie, dear, there must be a mistake." He feebly floundered. Why that would never happen to you. We can't afford it. The doctor is too far away. And furthermore, we don't have time, there's too much work to do."

"Yes, Ken," returned the pregnant partner, "I'm sure it's true and God will help us, and prayer will see us through, and I'm very happy over the prospect. Let's not worry about it."

Ken did worry about it however, and secretly, so did Dorthy. But the more they thought about it, the brighter became the prospect of their reproducing themselves into a new bundle of life. As both of them got over the embarrassment of talking about the coming event, they planned and discussed all the more about the arrival of this miracle baby. Ken became even more tender and caring over his bride, and the new little "laddie" that she was carrying inside of her. It never occurred to him that there was a 50% possibility of the "wee one" arriving as a "lassie".

The weeks sped by rapidly and soon the Kakwas became aware of a change in the appearance of the young Madame.

"Can it be true? they cackled around their evening fires, "that the white Madame will have a baby in the same manner that our Kakwa women have them? Maybe she's just getting fat on our manioc fufu."

As the Kakwas cackled, Ken became more and more concerned. How would he ever get her to Aba so she could be under Dr. Kleinschmidt's care? Then one morning she awakened feeling sicker than she had ever felt in all her life. This was not mere morning sickness. Her body burned with fever. This looked serious to Ken. He had seen and treated many cases like this among the Africans, and he was more apt to make proper diagnosis of this than he had in Dorthy's earlier morning sickness. This was an attack of malaria, and a very severe one. Dorthy had taken Quinine as a prophylaxis for the treatment. There was just no other way to treat it in those days.

But the fever did not break. Ken gave her as many liquids as she could take, but her body continued to burn with fever. Dollie was desperately sick. He called Akudri and the two of them resorted to their only recourse, prayer. The black man spoke softly and gently to Dollie "Nzambe azi! Nzambe azi! Ye Akuki!" (God is alive, and He will help you). He prayed over her as Ken looked on. Yoane went out and alerted the whole church. Little groups gathered in various places to pray.

Ken nursed the darling of his heart tenderly and lovingly, and very efficiently. Then one morning he noted that her urine was very dark. "Black Water Fever," he moaned, a disease of the kidneys where in the urine turns a blackish color, often caused by a reaction to the quinine treatment. It was very often fatal in those days, and especially so if there was not an experienced doctor on hand to treat it. Ken was beside himself with anxiety, but there were many Kakwas praying. His faith was strong. But what about the baby? Would he lose both of them? Or would God bring them both through it? Only God knew.

Akudri would come and sit at Dollie's bedside to give Ken opportunity to go to his trysting place near the ant hill. There he would prostrate himself and cry to God for deliverance. "Oh my God, if it be possible, let this cup pass from me". Thus he went through his own Gethsemane until he was finally able to finish the prayer of our Lord, "Nevertheless, not my will, but thine be done".

As he walked the red stone path back to his house, and his wife's bedside, he was weary. He had been close to his Lord, but the devil had been right there too to tempt him. "Your wife will die," mocked the monster, "and you will be left alone. You too will have black water fever but you won't have your Dollie to nurse you. You want to build a church here in Satan's territory. I'll show you who is the boss here."

But God spoke tenderly to his tormented treasure through familiar passages "Only believe -All things are possible." "It is I, be not afraid." "I will never leave thee, no! never will I forsake thee." Despite his weariness, he felt the burden was lifted. He shared it with Akudri, and both of them prayed a prayer of thanksgiving. Would he really be willing to let his young bride go, he faltered. But then he thought of his Savior in Gethsemane, and his resolve became firm. "Yes, Father," he prayed silently, "Thy will be done".

That night Dollie had a restful sleep. Her brow was cool. In the morning she awakened and was fully conscious. "Good morning, Ken," she said weakly, "where's my cup of tea?"

Ken was beside himself with joy and thanksgiving. Instead of the deathly pallor, there was a flare of color in her face. Her eyes were bright and the fever was gone. With a mischievous grin, she sipped her tea and nibbled a biscuit. A crisis had been passed, and Dollie was on the mend. "How good is the God we adore", hummed Ken as he began to nurse her back to health.

She was in her seventh month of pregnancy, and Ken's new worry was to get her to Aba. She still had fresh memories of the gruelling trip she had coming to Aba just a little over a year ago. God gave her fresh courage. The long tepoy trip was as cruel as the first one, but each night they slept well in a filthy Rest House along the way. Before they slept they prayed longingly that God would give them a healthy baby, be it Laddie or Lassie. Ken was reconciled to either now.

Dr. Kleinschmidt examined Dollie upon arrival. He secretly wondered whether the baby would be normal, or, indeed, if he would even make it. But he spoke encouragingly to the young couple. In a couple of weeks the little Lassie was born, and from all appearances both healthy and normal. She was their little bundle of Joy, and so they called her Joyce - born in 1926. They stayed for two months at Aba, and Coralee Kleinschmidt not only nursed them back to health, but she also gave Dorthy a good training in the art of changing and nursing the baby. But the young couple were anxious to get back to their beloved Kakwas at Adi, the place and people they had learned to love. But it would never do to take that little bundle of Joy on that long hot trip by tepoy. A new young missionary had just arrived, named Austin Paul, and he was to play a big part in getting mother and baby to Adi.

Austin had come on a motorcycle. Imagine, one of those daring, devilish devices on the Mission field. Most of the missionaries were shocked that a missionary would actually bring one of those mean monsters out with him, and entrust his body to the roaring ravages of its infernal and internal combustions.

But the contraption intrigued Dr. Kleinschmidt. Why could not Austin take the young mother and the baby in the side car all the way back to Adi? He broached the matter to Ken and the young mother. Dorthy hit the thatched roof. Never would she lend her body, nor that of her baby, Joycie, to this invention of the devil. The brash young American would be bad enough, but he with his motorcycle "Absolutely not!" she ejaculated. "Never will I allow my daughter to grow up with that on her conscience that she had ridden all the way to Adi on that mean obscene machine! That monster of Diablo! Never! and that's final."

"But Dollie, dear," soothed her husband, "how will you ever get home?" A quiet discussion followed in the privacy of their room. Dolly blew her patrician nose into her muslin handkerchief and dried her tears. Looking at her innocent little baby, she sighed, "Very well, Ken, dear, if there's no other way, lets get on with it."

Pragmatism prevailed. They packed the baggage they would need for the trip, and every precaution was taken for Joycies dangerous ride over the trails to Adi. Ken started immediately, so that he could have everything in readiness for Dollie's arrival. The mother and baby stayed with the Kleinschmidt's for another week.

D-day finally arrived for departure. Austin roared up with his Harley-Davidson. He was a real joker and a very "American" American, with cultural patterns that could be quite shocking to the aristocratic British lady. "O.K., Dollie," greeted the Yankee as he dismounted his still-smoking iron steed, "Lets ramble". "Imagine," thought Dorthy, "he scarcely knows me and he calls me 'Dollie'. He's taking liberties with the pet name that Ken has given me. 'Dollie' is Ken's special name". Her back stiffened and her voice was steel as she muttered her response. In a very undignified way she climbed into her side car. Doctor and Coralee handed the baby to her and bid them good-bye.

All settled and Austin jumped on the kick-starter. The machine belched out a roar. A good supply of clean diapers and baby necessities were tucked at Dollie's feet, and they were off. Dorthy was already worrying about nursing the baby in front of this young Yankee. Austin started the journey with enthusiasm. He was the hero, so he thought. But Ken must have been praying for them at that instant. Austin seemed to realize that he was in the driver's seat of a very delicate situation. He drove very carefully, slowing down for every bump, and carefully picking out the best parts of the road. Soon after the frightening start, Dorthy became accustomed to the jostling and jarring. Not all that bad, after all, she mused.

Austin looked down from his elevated perch to see if all was well. She caught his glance and rewarded him with a generous smile. That made the Yankee's day, and he became most chivalrous. After an hour jostling and jarring, Austin stopped the "pikipiki", as the Africans dubbed the mean obscene machine. "Time for a rest stop," he beamed at Dorthy. From then on he made hourly stops. They enjoyed Coralee's lunch together, and Dorthy was able to nurse her baby in comfort, while Austin discreetly absented himself for about 20 minutes. He "wanted to explore that swamp in the distance to see if there were any animals."

The trip was long and tiring, and one that Dorthy would never forget. Austin proved to be a real gentleman, and from that day on these two totally opposites were fast friends.

Ken was over joyed to see them arrive at Adi. Austin stayed around for a few days to help Ken get the station work going, while Ken spent much of his time helping Dorthy. They were greatly amused with the young Yankee. The Kakwas were extremely interested in little "Juicy", as they called the baby. They all wanted a close-up view of her, and they wanted to touch her. How could they make the little "mwana" feel at home without fondling her? This frightened the parents because of the many contagious diseases that were infectious. They made a strict "toli" (rule) that they could see but not touch. From early morning until night they flocked in from the surrounding villages to see "Juicy".

Ken must do something to control this. It was getting out of hand. He sent word to Chief Drupa that if they wanted to see the baby, they must come only on Sunday. The baby would be on display in the chapel, after the morning service. Ken was using a little trickery here, because the vast crowds never darkened the door of this chapel, but they did want to see "Juicy".

Sunday morning arrived, and before the crowing of the first cock, black feet were patting their way to Adi from miles around. Hundreds were crowding their way to Adi on the little narrow pathway. At 8:30 the drum was beaten, a signal for them to enter the chapel. The crowds pushed themselves inside, until the building was gorged with people. There was very little interest in the singing, or the prayers. Mrs. Richardson finally was ushered through the crowd by Akudri, who seated her on the platform. Nobody could come near until the service was finished.

"Kah! Kah! Kah!" they clucked after the preaching. This was really a show. Akudri formed the crowd into a single file, telling them strictly not to touch the baby, or to breathe on her face. For some three hours the white father, mother and infant stood on display. They were all totally exhausted. Yet they were very happy because wee Joycie was drawing crowds of people.

The following Sunday the program was repeated. Crowds poured in but they showed no interest in Ken's preaching or in Akudri's interpretation. Ken prayed much about the messages, so did Yoane. The little white phenomenon, "Juicy", was the attraction.

Gradually "Juicy" began to lose her popularity. Crowds still pressed in on Sundays, but the drawing card now was the "white father". His Bangala was not understood by most of the crowd, but Akudri was becoming a very efficient interpreter. The Holy Spirit was making plain the message, and pagans were beginning to see the light. The wily witch doctor was very angry because his credibility was beginning to fade, like a thunder cloud under the brightness of the sun.

The church was beginning to take root. Meanwhile "wee lassie" was developing very slowly. The mother's supply of milk was quite insufficient, and the parents made this a matter of real prayer. They felt that this was an attack of the Devil because that old Serpent seemed to understand that Joyce was to fill a very strategic role in the Kakwa church.

God answered the immediate problem by sending along Chief Drupa. He was as tall and ungainly as ever, and still gave the impression that he had just been awakened out of a Rip Van Winkle sleep. "Mbote, Bwana", greeted the chief, "how is Juicy?" The chief was shown the baby and he "Kah-Kahed" over her. He declared that she must have dropped to the earth from the silvery moon. "She is very nice, Madame," appraised the chief, "But she is too skinny. You must feed her some of our cow's milk. Very good, and rich cream. This would make your "Mwana" (baby) grow fat."

Ken only wished that he could buy some milk for the baby. The chief must have read his thoughts. "I will send Mite over with a gourd of milk every day." said the chief. More small talk, and an abundance of tea and 'biscuits' consumed, and the chief was gone.

The following day Mite showed up with a gourd of milk. Certainly not very sanitary, but rich in nourishing food value. Dorothy strained it with a flannel cloth, and the dirt strained out was unbelievable. She strained it again, and then again. She finally decided to boil it. Joycie began to grow.

A few days later a Belgian Official arrived by tepoy, followed by an entourage of soldiers and police. Several of the soldiers carried menacing and hippo-hide whips. The Belgian was invited into the Richardson home, where he and his Corporal were served tea. The Administrator too wanted to see the baby. He too remarked that the Petite was too skinny. "Mais non, Monsieur," replied Ken, "we don't actually have enough milk. Mite has promised to bring a supply but he is very irregular."

"Corporal," shouted the Belgian, "Go over to Mite's village and bring that lazy Kapita to me."

"Oui, Monsieur" snapped the Corporal with a salute. In about a half hour the Corporal came, leading Mite with a piece of rope which he had tied around his neck. "Kapita", growled the Belgian, "I understand that Drupa ordered you to bring milk everyday for this baby. Did you bring any today?"

Mite was ready with a lie, but a glimpse of Richardsons eye told him it was no use to lie. These white men were not to be trifled with. He dropped his eyes to the ground and said nothing.

"Speak up, you nyama (animal)! Did you or did you not bring milk today?"

"Kwanza te!" replied Mite weakly (not yet).

"Apisi ye mwambi! (Give him eight)" snorted the Belgian to the Corporal. The horrendous hippo-hide whip cut eight lashes into the bared buttocks of old Mite. The beleaguered black got up, sweating and with blood streaking down his legs, and saluted the Belgian.

"It's the only language that these animals understand," explained the Belgian to Richardson.

The missionaries were horrified at such treatment; however, from then on Mite delivered the milk daily, and with a good heart. He seethed with hatred for the white Belgian, but he was able to see that all whites are not alike. Mite became a good friend of the Mission. Joycie thrived on the milk. Akudri was growing in the Lord by leaps and bounds. The Richardsons were extremely happy in the work, for God had used the baby to break barriers, and win the hearts of the people. Prayer continued to play a great part in the development of the work, and Akudri was learning more and more "praying without ceasing". ❖

Akudri with his wife, Maria

Beautician with clients

# The Making of a Church
# Chapter 8

Missionaries have often been caricatured as colonialists who would exploit primitive peoples of a foreign culture. They have been maligned as paternalists who would destroy cultural patterns, and change the life-styles of undeveloped societies who don't want to be changed.

There are cultural patterns that are hazardous to the life and health of primitive societies. Bloodletting, for example, to allow sickness-causing spirits to escape from one's body — is a curse that has caused inestimable damage. The cruel form of circumcision imposed on girls reaching puberty has been responsible for permanent damage in the lives of many thousands. And on could go the list of perilous practices that are peculiar to the life style of many developing societies.

If members of missionary committees, elders and deacons of church boards, and especially Pastors could visit some of the mission fields of missionaries they support, they would be quicker to applaud the principles and practices of missions than to be appalled by them. They would understand the "reason" for missionaries in the early pioneer stages to act as paternalists; and why they must in the beginning serve as pastor of the newly appointed local church.

Before the organization of the local church at Adi the missionary was responsible for all the pastoral duties. He did most of the preaching, all of the marrying, discipling, and disciplining. But as the number of believers grew and became grounded in the Word, it was felt by the Mission that the Church should be organized locally. The eventual goal of such a local church was to become self-supporting, self propagating and self-governing. By the time the work at Adi was begun, the Africa Inland Mission was already well-established in Northeast Belgian Congo (now Zaire). They had arrived on the shores of Lake Albert near Kasengu in 1912. They had pressed north to Aba and then on to Dungu,

Aru, Aba and finally Adi. The latter, as we have seen, was opened by Jim Bell and Ralph Davis.

After the birth of Joyce Richardson, which God used as a drawing card to the inquisitive Kakwas, the number of believers grew rapidly. It was time to establish a locally organized church. George Van Dusen, the Congo Field Director, and Floyd Pierson, station superintendent of Aba station, came to Adi to help the Richardsons conduct the first Adi Church Conference. There were four believers who stood out as real leading men among the many others who had believed. They were Akudri, Konyuki, Owa and Rube. They were thoroughly examined by the missionaries as to their conversion, their doctrine, their walk, their devotional habits and their giving. They were approved for baptism - and on Sunday afternoon at a stream near the edge of the Adi Rock, Mr. Van Dusen baptized them in the presence of a multitude of black Kakwas, Lugbaras and Kaliko.

It was pagan custom to give their children names that had some pagan significance so it also became an established custom for Christians to choose a Bible name at their baptism. Akudri chose the name of Yoane (John). He had been impressed by John the Baptist with his stentorian voice, crying out in the wilderness the judgement of God. He had also been impressed by John the Apostle, who wrote affectionately, "My little children, these things write I unto you that ye sin not". Hence forth Akudri was known as Yoane, a man who came to be feared and revered throughout all of Zaire.

In those early days Yoane (as we shall designate him from here) worked faithfully as cook and general supervisor for the Richardsons. His work started by six A.M., with the first rays of sun peaking over the Adi Rock. He worked conscientiously until noon dinner was served. Afternoon was to cut his own garden, or to enlarge his house, or whatever — but Yoane used that time to canvass the surrounding villages. On a one-on-one basis, or in small groups under a shade tree, Yoane made plain the Path of Life. Every day he was out preaching with the zeal of a John the Baptist and the compassion of a John the Apostle. Thus many Kakwas were brought into the church.

There was, however, a missing dimension in Yoane's life. A need of which his own village brothers had been aware. One day they paid him a visit.

"Akudri," they greeted him, still using his old name, "We've come to talk to you about a personal need. — Don't you think it's time you were getting married? Here you are, a man of many dry seasons, and still no children. It is time for you to buy a wife — and to start a family." Yoane was glad to see his brothers. It had been a long time. He asked about the beautiful Kitoko, his step mother, and all the others. He shared with them the good news that concerned himself, his growth in the Lord, his baptism and his new name.

"Yes, my brothers," he finally came back to the main subject, "It's time that I must search out a wife for myself. If we, sons of Dada, are going to perpetuate his name, then we cannot allow his genes to die in our loins. I have been thinking a good deal of marriage lately."

They discussed the matter of dowry and the availability of family wealth. If Yoane's tastes would not be too high, they could afford a wife, but not for more than 5 cows. Yoane would have to be tough with the man who was going to be his father-in-law.

They had a good lengthy visit punctuated by a number of gutsie laughs. Yoane had prayer with them, remembering each member of his clan by name, imploring God in his trumpet voice that each one of his household would be saved. — After a tasty feast the brothers were gone.

Yoane was often found near the Zeriba (Girls' School Compound) looking through the fence, into the "Promised Land". He was on the lookout for the right woman. Her looks would be important, for Yoane had an appreciation of aesthetic values. - However there were more important qualities. She must be a Christian who would place Christ as the first priority in her life. She must know how to cook a good meal, keep her home and garden in perfect condition, and it would help if she would have a sense of humor. — It would be extremely important that she have a good healthy body that could bear healthy children for him. Also do the heavy work of fetching water on her head, cutting the firewood and cutting the garden. Outside of the basic qualities, he dreamed, he would not be hard to please.

With such cogitations he made daily excursions to the Girls' Zeriba to spy out the land. There were 5 different females who looked attractive to him. And there was one further, one not living in the Zeriba, but over at the nearby village of Kapita Mite. Her name was Libi and she was a very nice person, meeting all of Yoane's demands except for the fact that her body was very small and slender. She would never be able to do the work he had in mind for her, and her hips, though very shapely, were no where near wide enough for her to bear the sons and daughters he had in mind. He had better go back to one of the original 5 at the Zeriba.

One day when he was spying in the Zeriba, he saw one of his choice candidates getting very angry at another girl. She was shouting and acting very unchristian. If she treated one of her classmates that way, what would she ever do to a husband? She was crossed off the list forthwith.

Another, he discovered, was hopeless as a cook. Still another, he found out was untruthful. She told little "white" lies with impunity. And a fourth one of his possibilities was hopelessly lazy. She would never do. — This left only one to propose to. — The black preacher liked this girl very much. She stood tall, and walked like an African Queen. Her strong body rippled with muscles, a very athletic and pleasing type, strong as a young heifer. Her face was beautiful, as though carved out of an ebony block by a master sculptor. She was thick of thigh, and with busts that were bulging—ideal for bearing a good number of healthy sons. Perhaps a few daughters as well that could be sold to acquire dowry wealth for the sons. He liked the looks of this biggy, and he felt that he was ready to propose to her.

But Yoane being the man of prayer that he was, would certainly want to pray over the decision. Pray he did, and very seriously. — The more he prayed, and the more he reflected on his fabulous female, the less he was inclined to sleep that night. If only he could get that feeling of peace that he usually experienced after a session of prayer, he would feel great. But whenever he thought of this beautifully busted black beauty - a vision of Libi, the slim little slip with the sleek, slick figure, flashed before him. It seemed that God was directing the young Romeo to this little Juliet.

Yoane was perplexed as he deliberated his dilemma. The biggy had so many pluses. — But as he thought about Kapita Mites' daughter a vision of her face appeared and was beautiful, no doubt about it.- But better than physical beauty, Libi had many more pluses to present.— Yoane knew that this young woman dearly loved her Lord, and she faithfully studied His Word. She prayed more earnestly. True her lithesome limbs were slender and showed little promise of ever doing a day's heavy work in the garden. Would she ever be able to carry his sons in such little loins? - Could this really be God's choice?

Not until the young preacher was ready to acknowledge Libi as God's choice did he have a peaceful nights sleep. He asked various ones who knew Libi about her character, her disposition, her faithfulness in her garden work. He even found an ant hill behind which he could hide in order to spy on her work. Every prospect was pleasing to Yoane, and he made a decision. He would propose to her the next afternoon when he was sure he would find her alone in the manioc garden.

Late in the afternoon he saw her coming out of her garden. He accosted her with "Mbote mingi, Libi. Sango nini?" (a very good evening, Libi. How are you?)

"Mbote mingi, Yoane," was her bashful response. She looked like a cornered deer that was frantically searching an escape. But Yoane had business with her and he was not about to let his prize slip away. He stood square in her path, and it would have been very rude for her to sneak past him and run away.

"How is your body, Libi? Is it in good health?" pursued the pursuer awkwardly. He was never at a loss for words, but this business of proposing to a woman was something else. He was definitely not a romanticist, nor was Libi. Things weren't going according to plan, but Yoane was determined. He had started, and he was not about to abandon his pursuit.

"Libi, I love you. Will you marry me?" he blurted out. This was not at all the speech he had planned the night before as he lay sleeplessly on his sleeping mat. He thought that he had memorized such a romantic and appropriate proposal that would have swept her off her feet and into his arms. It had eluded him. He had blown it for sure. But he had popped the question and now there was nothing to do but wait for an answer.

Libi stood before him with eyes glued on the path. The skin on her face was a brilliant black. Black skins have a hard time blushing so she was spared that embarrassment. Her only clothes were the inevitable bouquet of leaves in front of her quivering body, and another behind her. She fidgeted from one foot to another and nervously plucked one of the fresh green leaves from her waist. How on earth was she supposed to answer this question? No doubt about her wanting to accept Yoane's invitation, but how to say it?

Finally, with eyes directly focused on Yoane's, she spoke the only words she could think of —"Azi kula na yo" (It's your affair). The answer didn't sound right to her, but Yoane took it as her acceptance. "Oh, Merci na Nzambe, — Merci!" (Oh, thanks to God. Thanks to you).

He let out a yell that scared a whole family of monkeys scampering up a distant tree as though the whole forest were on fire. Yoane leaped high into the air as though he'd been shot through the heart with a hunter's arrow. The hunter being cupid, and the pierced heart was that of both of them. Yoane ran as fast as he could, leaping over bushes and scattering chickens and goats that were in his path, all the way to Bwana Richardson's house—where he and his wife were enjoying their "Sun Downer", which was a strong cup of tea. "Oh Bwana! - Oh Madame," he exclaimed breathlessly, "Good News! I have asked Libi, the daughter of Mite to marry me and guess what! - She has agreed!"

The Richardsons were exceedingly happy about this news, hadn't they been praying about this daily? They poured Yoane a cup of tea, for which he had developed a real taste. Richardson began to extol the virtues of marriage. Hadn't he and Dollie experienced a kind of bliss that was as close to heaven as one could possibly find this side the pearly gates? They counselled the romantic young preacher, and had a prayer of thanksgiving as well as for guidance for the young couple. Even Bwana himself, who had been too busy for romance lately had a wistful look in his eye as he stole a glance at his own young wife.

Ken had his workmen build a neat mud and wattle hut that had 3 rooms in it. They put a thick layer of thatch that would keep the rain outside, and not allow it to leak into the house of the lovers. — Their romantic spirits must not be dampened. There were proper doors that were hung on proper hinges that had been imported from Belgium, and proper wooden shutters at the windows. A veritable honeymoon cottage, neatly white washed inside and out.

In due course the dowry was legally settled, and Yoane paid the bride's father 5 cows, and two goats thrown in for good measure. — After all, Libi was worth an extra gift, and this made the Kapita, Mite look favorably on his new son-in-law. They were married in 1926 in the chapel that was about ready to burst its mud walls to make room for the crowds.

Libi was a number of years younger than Yoane and very petite, but she took her place as Yoane's one and only wife. No longer did he cherish the ambition with which he once taunted his old step-father, namely that he would one day have six wives. He had eyes only for Libi. She pleased him in every way, and she was growing in the Lord.

About two years after their marriage, Libi appeared before the elders of the young church to be examined as a candidate for baptism. She was catechized thoroughly as to her faith in Christ, her witnessing to others, her conduct and her giving. She was baptized in 1928, and she chose the name "Maria". From then on she was known as "Maria na Yoane" (Maria the wife of Yoane).

Their life together (64 years to date) has been a beautiful example of matrimonial bliss. They are still in love. — Only once, about fifty-five years ago, there was a ripple on the sea of matrimony. Yoane lost his cool. — At their wedding a missionary had given them a bright enamel cooking pot, —

a big one. They both thought it very beautiful. — Yoane gave her strict instruction that this was not to be taken to the stream to be used as a water pot. This was to be used only in the house.

One day Maria could not find an empty earthen water pot to go and fetch water. The enamel pot, still shiny and beautiful, sat appealingly on a shelf. Maria's eyes fell on it. — Why not use this only once, until she could get another earthen pot. Not only did she look, but she took the pot. As one might guess, Yoane met the guilty gal on the path with the forbidden pot balanced gracefully on her head.

Nothing was said on the path, but once they were inside their hut a scene took place. — Yoane exploded, "How could you?" further harsh words followed. Maria spilled some "mai-misu" (tears) over her ebony cheeks. A morose mood pervaded their home for several hours. Finally Yoane began to realize that he had not reacted as Christ would have done.

"Maria, my dear mwasi," he said sadly, "I spoke to you in a very bad manner. After all, that pot is yours as much as it is mine. If you need it to fetch water you have every right to use it. Will you please forgive me?"

Embraces, fondlings and caresses soothed their wounded spirits. They exchanged expressions of love and fit right back into their harmonious and compatible life style. "Maria na ngai" (My Maria) is how he often refers to her in a sermon illustration, and that's what he called her again on that occasion. Maria was a faithful wife, and never once since that isolated little scenario, has there been a harsh word between them.

God blessed their union with a large family. The fruitful vine that God referred to figuratively in Psalm 128 produced ten little olive plants. Like some other preachers' families, some of the boys were a grief to the parents. Some one has observed that, "the reason the preachers kids are the worst kids is because they play with your kids", Davidi, their oldest, in whom they had such great aspirations, turned to a dissolute life. For years the grief-stricken parents prayed for their prodigal son. Several years before his death, at about 35 years of age, the prodigal said in his heart, "I will arise and go home". He arose, and he went. He confessed his sinful life to his father and to his God. He served the Lord faithfully with his father for about two years, until a very virile disease took his life.

Davidi's repentance was a great joy to the parents, and caused them to pray even more persistently for others who had followed the elder son in his path of perfidy. ❖

Running water

## The Making Of A Pastor
## Chapter 9

The Church at Adi was growing at a remarkable rate. Always it seemed that Mission personnel was inadequate to assign more than one couple to Adi for church work. Ken Richardson needed help in the vast amount of planting and building churches in the surrounding villages. Yoane was still cook for Mrs. Richardson, but his work as evangelist and preacher was encroaching more and more of his time.

Mission leaders appraised the work at Adi and evaluated their needs. God seemed to indicate only one solution for the personnel problem. A solution which would prove to be strategic in the establishment of a sound indigenous church. The conclusion was that Yoane should be ordained as a minister, and that he should give his full time to pastoral work.

At that time there were still no ordained African Pastors in the Africa Inland Church in Zaire. When the field Council met they felt that God would have them set a precedent by ordaining Yoane. "Let's take a bold step," they decided, "and get some qualified African pastors into places of leadership."

A committee of missionaries along with some church elders from various parts of the field arrived at Adi to make church history. They examined Yoane thoroughly as to his knowledge of the Word. At this juncture he had not yet studied in the Bible Institute which was under the direction of Dr. Harry Stam.

However, the committee discovered that he had remarkable insight into the Scriptures. He was examined in detail regarding his study habits, his personal and family devotions, his conversion and his call into the ministry, his tithing, relationships with missionaries and fellow-believers, his marriage and family.

"Do you ever quarrel with your wife?" — asked the Committee. At this question Yoane hung his head in shame. His eyes were downcast, and the large blood vessel in his neck began to pulsate visibly. Drops of sweat appeared on his brow.

"Yes, my brothers, I did once have a serious quarrel with my wife," he confessed shamefully. "I am thoroughly ashamed of it. It was about a beautiful enamel cooking pot that was given to us as a wedding present and we had a serious argument. I became very angry. Maria has long since forgiven me, but I will never forgive myself for treating my dear wife as I did. It was all my fault."

When the Committee had exhausted their stream of questions to Yoane, they called in Maria. They catechized her almost as thoroughly as they had Yoane. —At last came the loaded question, "How do you get along with your husband? Do you ever quarrel with him?"

Maria recoiled as though a hippo hide whip had lashed her across the face. Her spirit was draped in shame. After regaining a semblance of composure she responded, "Yes, my brothers, once soon after we were married we met on the path to the water hole; and we quarrelled shamefully. You see, it was like this," and she poured out in doleful detail the account of the enamel pot. She told the story exactly as Yoane had told it with only one point differing, "Yoane has forgiven me. It was all my fault," she concluded, placing the whole blame on her own two shapely shoulders.

The Council considered carefully all the aspects of the interviews. This was an important, historic step. They must not make a mistake. They sought the Lord earnestly in prayer, before making a decision. When they polled the members they discovered that they were in unanimous agreement in their desire to lay their hands on Yoane's head to pray over him, and set him apart as a minister of the Gospel.

Like Paul, the Apostle, Yoane has been a minister of Christ whose labors were abundant, with painful persecutions. He knew what it was to be beaten and buffeted, and to be thrown into a rat and vermin infested jail. On more than one occasion he was shot at, and given an unfair "Peoples-Court" trial, conducted by haters of Christ and His Church. Some of these experiences will be related in a later chapter.

Again like Paul, Yoane's greatest agony was a thorn in the

flesh. This painful infirmity in his body had its origin during the days of his youth, when he was still a slave to the devil. It had been his desire, and also that of his family, that he should be the "King of the Dance" for his whole Clan. — In order to look the part he must have his ears pierced so that he could wear the heavy copper ringlets in his ear lobes. These would jingle as he danced. They made him look very impressive in his role, but the affect on his ears was devastating.

The result was that both his ears became badly infected. For many months these wounds suppurated profusely, and pained him night and day. After his conversion he jettisoned the jingling janglers, and his sores finally healed up. There remained however, an ugly growth of scar tissue under each ear lobe which eventually formed into keloidal growths, about the size of golf balls.

Dr. Kleinschmidt at the Aba hospital examined these when he was once at the Aba Hospital on a preaching mission. Riding his bicycle over 85 miles of very rough paths had caused much jarring and jostling of these two meat balls. This caused them to bleed and eventually become infected again. — The doctor decided that he would do something about it. He neatly excised both the growths, and then took layers of skin from his upper legs. — He did a beautiful job of cosmetic surgery and skin grafting. The process was painful, but Yoane was not one to complain.

For several years he looked fine, but alas, the scar tissue started to grow into keloids again. Slowly at first — but relentlessly, on both sides of his face, they finally developed into larger meat balls than before. Yoane was depressed about this for a while, but his debonair disposition would not allow self-pity for long. This was his cross to bear, and bear it he would with buoyancy.

Dr. Becker later examined him and took him to the Oicha hospital, some 300 miles from Adi. He too operated on him with the same successful results, and the same initial encouragement. But alas, in another year or so they began to grow again, and this time into the size of large grapefruits. Dr. Ted Williams from Uganda operated on him too. — In all, these three doctors operated on Yoane seven times, each one very painful, but looking promising. —Each time they started to grow again.

In the early seventies Yoane was invited to preach in many of the larger churches in America and Canada. During that trip, Peter Stam, the A.I.M. Home director in Canada at that time took Yoane to a specialist in Toronto. The doctor was sure there would be a miracle drug that could dissolve these ungainly growths. After another cosmetic surgery, the doctor gave Yoane about 70 injections all along the areas of his ear lobes and his neck. The treatment was drastic and painful — but God used it to work a miracle. For years the scars did not re-appear.

In the early eighties, however, the scar tissue started to grow again, ever so slightly. The growth seemed to continue only for a short time, so that at present he has only very slight keloidal growths behind his ears. — The scars are still there, and his appearance still causes people to stare at him. But Yoane is completely oblivious to the stares and stage whispers about his "matuas" (ears).

When Edythe and I were living at Adi during the late forties, we sent him to Oicha Hospital for one of his three operations that Dr. Becker performed on him. A month later we went to Oicha to bring him back home. We found him with his head swathed in bandages, and he was very quiet all the way home.

The next morning, back at Adi, we walked over to his house to see how he was getting along. We found him sitting on a little "Kiti pala" (small stool for women) under a mango tree, a picture of dejection. He held his head in his hands, all stooped over, and paying no attention to us.

"Mbote mingi, Yoane," we greeted him. "We are very sorry to see you with so much pain."

"Oh Bwana," he moaned in return. "Yes, my ears are paining me. But there's another pain that is far worse, and it is something that I cannot bear." Tears were streaming down his face.

"That pain is not of my ears. Dr. Becker gave me a good operation, and though it is painful, yet I can bear that gladly.

But the pain that is killing me is the pain in my heart." Clasping his heart, he continued, "My heart is broken for my son. Oh, my son! — He has fallen into gross sin, and has brought reproach to the heart of my Father in heaven. The pain of my ears is nothing in comparison to the pain of my heart. My son is killing me."

A broken-hearted father, weeping over an erring son. This is his real "thorn in the flesh". The scars on his face are a rare source of physical pain to him now. — In fact, he uses them as an opening to give his testimony for what Christ has done in his life. ❖

Women's Conference at Watsa

# The Stuff of the Preacher
## Chapter 10

"To Preach, Oh Lord, give me the stuff, and nudge me when I've said enough."

This preacher's prayer has been prayed faithfully by Yoane through the years. The Lord has been giving him the necessary "stuff", but has not yet given him the "nudge". Starting on a one-on-one basis of personal evangelism, and developing into a leader of small groups meeting under trees, or on verandas of some of the larger houses, he has been preaching the Gospel for over 65 years.

Necessity is laid upon me; yea, woe is me if I preach not the Gospel. I Cor. 9:16

The whole story of Yoane's life, his struggle with meningitis, his deliverance from the witch doctor, his being divinely nudged away from the position of dance leader and finally, his being catapulted into the national lime light of Zaire, all blends a beautiful background for a very colorful preacher.

It was too good to keep to himself. Unless he could share these blessings, along with the Gospel message, he would be thoroughly frustrated. Preaching was what God called him to do, and it mattered little to him who his audience might be. Often they were the sick in any of the Missions' hospitals. They could be a large crowd of bawling barefoot pagans at an open graveside with the remains of a loved one. It might be to a lonely barefooted, bare-breasted African woman, balancing a basket of beans on her head on the way to the Market. It might be a woman at the waterhole filling her water pot. It could even be a bellicose Belgian Official on safari through the area, scaring the wrath of God into whole villages. His auditors might be children on the way to school, or a goat-herder, guarding his ungainly goats.

Without distinction Yoane regarded each individual as an eternal being that would spend eternity either in bliss with the Savior, or in blackness of Satan's hell. Nor did tribal distinction enter into his thinking. He preached to Lugbaras, Kakwas, British, or Belgian, prince or pagan, poor or pecuniary. They were all his evangelistic responsibility.

In his early years his evangelistic zeal was spent largely on the Kakwas. But the Lord spoke to him through a verse of scripture that was burned into his heart. It was: "And other sheep have I which are not of this zeriba. Them also I must bring, and they shall hear my words. There shall be ONE Zeriba, and ONE Watcher of the sheep."

Yoane knew that there were many other tribes. "Them also I must bring", was the axiom of his burning heart. Tribalism was absolutely forbidden in the Shepherd's church. "One Zeriba."

His one on one personal evangelism reached out to other tribes. But with his voluminous voice that could easily be heard at the extremity of the largest crowds, Yoane had the natural ability to be a great preacher. That, coupled with a burden for lost souls and a deep commitment to Christ, he had the necessary stuff. And where could he find a more perfect outlet than at the public market.

Every Wednesday morning crowds of men, women and children would slap their bare feet on the iron-stone path leading to Drupa's village. For miles they came in little family units. The father always led the pack of one or two or more wives, depending on how rich he was, or whether he was a member of the church.

Children came too to buy and sell small wares at the market. The men came in a freshly washed loin cloth tucked under a cowhide belt tied around their naked hips. They wore sandals made out of buffalo skins with deer skin straps attached to keep them on their feet. As a status symbol, a few of the men wore a hat. It might be an old pith helmet, battered and torn. It was often far too big for the man, completely covering his ears. This prize may have been a cast off of a Belgian Official or a Greek merchant. To complete his attire, the man would swagger a beautifully carved walking stick, usually made from a branch cut from a mahogany tree; whittled down to a shapely size. It shone brightly from the generous application of a palm-oil polish.

The women's apparel for this gala day was less expensive

than the men's, but far more glaring and flaring. There was no costly cloth involved for most of them. They merely washed their bodies thoroughly, and applied generous amounts of palm fat which they rubbed into their skins until their naked bodies gleamed with a glossy glow. After the ablutions and the luster of the Palm fat they wove large bunches of fresh green manioc leaves into shapely bouquets. If their husbands were prosperous they supplied their wives with a generous amount of multi-colored beads. These they wove artistically into beautiful belts which they wore gracefully around their naked thighs. The manioc leaves were tucked underneath, a bunch in the front to cover their groin and another in the rear to cover their behinds. The rest of their luminous body was exposed to the elements. No one, except for the lusty-eyed Belgians and the Greek merchants took notice of their beautifully carved breasts. Missionaries used to look at the tree tops until they had been there for a number of months. Then they became quite unaware of them. At least that's the way it was supposed to be.

The most important detail of the woman's get-up was her coiffure. This took several hours the evening before market day. Her first task was to wash her hair thoroughly. Then the hairdresser took over and her first step was to look for lice. If she found a few little eggs, and a few baby creatures, she didn't make a fuss. If there was a big family of them she would simply take a razor-sharp knife and shave off all of the hair. Only a bright shiny dome remained. There would be no cute coiffure until her hair would grow in again - free of lice.

If there were no lice found the hairdresser parted the kinky hair into narrow sections that stood straight up. There would be about six or eight of these sections with straight parts between. The Dresser wove these into tight little braids, starting each section at the front hairline and working back to the neck. By the time she was finished she had a very ornamental head of carefully coiffed curls. The process took several hours, but it was time well spent, the girls thought. The prima donna was a beauty to behold.

Coiffure completed, the girl would search for several bunches of flowers picked from jacaranda trees and bougainvillaea and hibiscus bushes. At certain seasons of the year there were beautiful orchids and violets growing in the fields after the first rains began to fall. Colors of every tint and tinge, tone and tincture, were displayed in these little bouquets fastened into their braids and ear lobes. Flowers of every shade were a must for every female whether married or single, fat or flimsy, pregnant or wasp-waisted. They felt naked without flowers. If a family of lice had been responsible for a shiny dome she would wear a garland of flowers around her neck.

Boys not yet having reached the age of pubescence went to the market just as they were - i.e. in their birthday suits. Sometimes as they marched to the market in groups they sang hymns. Not infrequently these little nudists sang "Just as I am, without one plea". They of course were singing of their spiritual condition. Missionaries, however, could not help but smile as they gazed at the little marchers "just as they were". I am convinced that God's sense of humor must have surfaced, too, at the sight of this parade.

By 9:00 A.M. the large field near the chief's compound was swarming with black people. The wives of the wealthy wore gay pieces of colorful calico, gracefully wrapped around their figures. Their head-kerchiefs, worn saucily, represented all the colors of the rainbow.

Men gathered around the large earthen pots containing some fifteen gallons of a powerful home-brewed liquid they called "MASANGA". The wives had brewed the stuff and they were in charge of the "bar", which was simply an array of these large filthy pots. Each woman had a supply of small gourds holding a pint each. She dipped it into the great pot and sold it to the ever-increasing line of customers for 50 centimes, or about 1/3 of a cent. The customer would bolt down his pint of fire water in one breathless gulp and hand it back for a refill. The gourd was passed from one filthy mouth to another without ever a thought of washing it.

By noon there was a crowd of rabble-rousers were stenchfully stewed. These were always a threat to the peaceful conduct of the market. If there were enough sober soldiers around, they would drag the worst disturbers to the bloc.

At 10:00 Yoane arrived on his bicycle, going to the very center of the market, a safe distance from drunken debauchery of the beer-bibbing boozers at the side of the market. He was followed by a number of other Christian cyclists who had Christian literature, their bibles and hymn books, and a few trumpets tied on their luggage carriers. Some of the men had been taught to play the instruments by a simple number system.

These leaders gathered in a small circle and began to play and sing several songs. As soon as the first notes of the trumpets pierced the noise of the crowd the hubbub of buying and selling ceased. The crowds quit moving around and sat down beside their displays of merchandise. Several thousand sat down reverently on the ground and sang along with Yoane as he led the singing. After several songs there was a prayer.

The majority of the crowd were of the Kakwa tribe, but there was also a sizable portion — perhaps a fourth of them — who were Lugbaras. Without an interpreter this large segment would not understand the message. Yoane, in his vehement voice, would read a passage of Scripture in Bangala which would then be read in Lugbara by his interpreter. In the sermon Yoane would preach in succinct sentences in Kakwa. While he regained his breath his interpreter shot the identical contents concisely and accurately into Lugbara. For about twenty minutes these two preachers would seesaw back and forth in staccato sentences, spelling out the Gospel message. The sermon was dramatically delivered, and graphically illustrated. Yoane is a born Actor and knows how to make the sermon alive. But the factor of greatest importance was that the Holy Spirit was in control. The crowd loved the sermon. Through the years literally thousands of souls have been brought to the Savior at these market meetings.

Before 1960 Zaire was the Belgian Congo, under strict, and often brutal control. It was officially known as a Catholic Country, and the Roman Church was the State

Church. All branches of Protestantism were regarded as heretical. It was through diplomatic negotiations on the international level that Protestant Missions were tolerated.

Through the personal friendship that existed between the early General Director of AIM, the Reverend Charles Hurlburt, and the President of the United States, pressure was brought to bear on the Belgian Government regarding Protestants. Belgium could ill-afford to lose favor with their benevolent ally, the avuncular Uncle Sam, by disregarding a request from the President. Theodore Roosevelt had asked the Belgians to allow AIM missionaries to enter the Colony as bona fide missionaries with all rights and courtesies. This was during the first decade of the twentieth century.

With letters from both President Roosevelt and King Leopold II of Belgium AIM missionaries entered the Congo in 1912. "International diplomacy not withstanding, the Congo was still a Catholic country. When the priests from the Aru area saw Yoane's very successful evangelistic meetings at the markets, with scores of conversions each month, they were understandably perturbed.

The Pere Superieure made it a point to be there on a Wednesday morning to see what was going on. The reverence shown by the Kakwas and Lugbaras as they sang the hymns in languages that both tribes could understand, and the effective use of the trumpets was amazing to the priest. To hear Yoane preach so forcefully and intelligently through an interpreter, communicating the Gospel most effectively was unbelievable. It was just too much for the priest. Nor did he fail to be impressed by the harvest of souls that accepted the Savior. He not only admired what he saw, but he was also deeply concerned. After all, Congo was a Catholic Country. What he was seeing at this market indicated clearly that the Kakwa tribe was predominantly Protestant. How had they ever gotten such a foot-hold. He would have to make a Catholic convert out of Yoane. He would sweet-talk him into it. What was that proverb about catching more flies with honey?

He went to Yoane directly after the last hymn was sung. In a very friendly manner (too friendly, thought Yoane) he made a lot of small talk. "There is only one God Yoane, whether we worship him as Catholics or as Protestants."

Yoane agreed, but he asked the Priest some hard questions concerning the new birth, and confessing our sins directly to God, and what saving value there was in the various sacraments. Yoane was always polite, and always graceful, but never once allured by the attractive offers of the Father.

The Catholic cleric soon found out that Yoane knew just as much about the New Testament as he did, and that he was not going to be easily persuaded. But the priest was also a poker player. He had another card up his sleeve. If tempting tactics failed, he would try another tactic. This preacher, Yoane, was a danger to the Congolese Government. With his kind of influence he could easily incite a rebellion. And even more serious, in the eyes of the cleric, he was making a protestant tribe out of the very progressive Kakwa people. The following Sunday the Government Administrator, a Catholic, came to attend mass at the Catholic Mission. After mass the Priest invited the official to the Mission Mess hall to have dinner with him. The official was wined and dined, and then provided with a savory cigar.

"Mon cher Fils (My dear Son)" began the Priest as he lit up his costly cigar, "You have a very serious problem on your hands with the Kakwas. There is a Pastor named Yoane Akudri at the Adi Mission who is a real trouble maker. He is a very dangerous man. He can sway an audience of 2000 people at the Chief's Market. He makes all the people stop their buying and selling, there by interfering with the market.

The priest went on to explain what he saw at the Market. "They sing lewd songs that sound like slogans against the Government. With his loud voice, he controls the people. He prates like a prophet of heresy. He will certainly lead the whole tribe into an insurrection."

The Administrator listened with amazement to this harangue. He knew Yoane well as he had visited the missionaries at Adi. He had drunk tea with Yoane, and found him to be a very amicable friend. He had grown very fond of him thinking of him as a very good leader, and loyal to the Government.

"Mais non, Mon Pere. Vous devez etre tort" (But no, My Father, you must be mistaken), responded the official, blowing a massive whiff of blue cigar smoke to blend in with the aromatic cloud that already filled the room. "I have met Yoane and I always find him very polite. I know of his faithful work as a pastor at Adi. Even though he is not a Catholic, he is a good man."

The Priest was not accustomed to being contradicted. His complexion became apoplectic, and his attitude pugnacious. "You listen to me, my son, that man Yoane is a

knave in the church and a menace to the Government. He is capable of starting a rebellion. I'm warning you plainly. You better take steps to get rid of him. If you don't, then you yourself may find your position in jeopardy."

So that was it. The official knew that the priest had just that much political clout that he could pull it off. He could have him relegated to some remote desert place in the country. He would have to be very careful not to make an enemy of this church man.

"I will investigate the matter, Mon Pere," replied the subdued official meekly. He still thought Yoane was O.K., and that the Priest was making a big mistake. However, he would have to be diplomatic if he wanted to pursue his career. "I shall take the proper measures." This whole event was taking place in the 1940's when Edythe and I were stationed at Adi. On a Wednesday morning soon after the Priest had confronted the Administrator, we received an excited delegation of Church leaders. "Yoane is in prison at Drupa's village! They haven't beaten him yet, but they surely will. The Bulamatadi said that Yoane is to be deported."

Sweat was exuding from all the pores of these excited believers, and they were puffing like a steam engine. There was only one thing to do. We all got into our station wagon and drove over to Drupa's village on the double. We met the chief who confirmed the reports. The Bulamatadi was going to deport the Pastor.

Following the chief we knocked at the Guest House door. The Belgian was just finishing his lunch of sardine sandwiches. He greeted us cordially, "Please come in, Monsieur Brashler, and seat yourselves. I'll have the boy bring you some tea."

Rather non-plussed, we accepted the invitation. How were we going to handle this very difficult situation? It was obvious to see that he was doing this to Yoane under duress. The tea he served was not the best. Belgians were connoisseurs of coffee, but not of tea. We took care of the amenities.

"Monsieur l'Administrateur", I began with a bit of embarrassment, "I'm sure you know why I am here. Is it true that you have Yoane locked up in jail, and that you are intending to send him away?"

The Administrator was not going to enjoy this part of our visit, "Monsieur Brashler," he began nervously, "I don't know what to say. I have heard that Yoane interferes with the market, stopping the people from buying and selling. He has far too much influence with the Kakwa people - more so than I myself do. It is felt by the functionaires of the Government that Yoane is a threat to the Government and that it would be in the best interests of all to send him away. But I promise you, Monsieur, we will send him to Katanga Province which has a very good climate. He and his family can start all over new. He will have perfect liberty."

"But," I objected, "Are you going to deport him without a trial. Certainly, you enlightened Belgians would not take such drastic action".

"Oh, mais certainement, Monsieur, Yoane will have a hearing. In fact, I will send for him right now".

The Pastor was marched into the Guest House between two armed guards. He looked as sharp as though he were ready to step into the pulpit not one bit perturbed. He spoke to me in Kakwa which the Belgian did not understand, "Mboto, Bwana, like the Apostle Paul, I am a prisoner of Jesus Christ, Hallelujah."

The official was astounded at his composure, and at his "hallelujah", the only word he understood. How was he going to manage this? He resolved that a kind and positive approach would be the best. He had great admiration for this fearless and fine looking black man.

"Pastor Yoane," he began cautiously, "I'm sorry that I have had to put you in jail. However, it has been brought to my attention that you are interfering with the Wednesday markets."

He went on to enumerate the complaints that he had against him. "For that reason the Government officials feel that you should move to the Katanga Province. There we will give you a nice parcel of land with a good house on it. You can start all over new with your family."

"Merci, Monsieur," Yoane's politeness and diplomacy were some of his good qualities, "But may I ask you a question? Where did you get all of this information about me?" The official blushed with embarrassment. "From the Pere at the Catholic Mission," was his abashed response.

"I see," said Yoane, and waited quietly for a dramatic moment. I sat amazed. "Some trial" I thought, "Without asking any questions and without giving him an opportunity to defend himself. The case is all drawn and quartered."

Yoane was not in the least disturbed, "I want to thank you too, Monsieur, for not giving me the whip. Almost every one who is put into jail is given the whip. You have spared me this but if you would have given me the hippo hide fimbo, I would have thanked you for it. It would have been an honor for me to take a whipping like my Lord did."

"As to your sending me away from my people, that will be perfectly all right with me, I have spent many years with my Kakwa people, and I have had ample opportunity to preach the Gospel to them. There is a large church at Adi with over one thousand members. They are strong in the Lord. There will be dozens of strong pastors who will take my place."

"In fact I will welcome a change of country. All the Kakwas know me - I have preached to all of them. Many have accepted my Lord as their Savior. I want to go to a new territory to preach. This Gospel is not for the Kakwas only - it is for all of the Congolese to hear."

"It is even for you, Monsieur. You too must confess your

sins to Christ, and believe that Jesus is Lord and that only His death can cover your sins. If you don't you will be lost for all eternity, in spite of your sacraments and your being a Catholic. That is the only way to heaven."

All through this long speech the Administrator listened quietly with deep respect. God had spoken to him through this black Pastor. He was profoundly impressed and also mellowed.

He turned to me and said, "Monsieur Brashler, I've never heard anything like this before. Your Pastor is a real man of God. I cannot be responsible for sending him away."

He dismissed the soldiers and finally spoke to Yoane, "Pastor Yoane, I don't think your work here is finished. I believe that God wants you to stay here."

"But what about my trip to Katanga?" teased Yoane mischievously, "I am ready to go if you want to send me."

The official laughed and shook hands with the Pastor. To me he said in French, "You have a wonderful man of God in your Pastor".

I agreed with him heartily and said, "In no way will he be a threat to the Government. You should hear him preach to his congregation from Romans 13, urging them to be obedient to the "powers that be," and to give "honor to whom honor is due".

The Administrator stayed in the territory for many years in spite of the fact that he acted in a way contrary to the wishes of the Priest. His friendship with Yoane continued to grow more cordial.

Even the priest came to respect Yoane as a man of God. On certain occasions they were together as guests at social functions. The Catholic cleric, like Yoane, had a mischievous sense of humor.

"Pastor Yoane, won't you join me in drinking a toast to our work?"

"Non, Mon Pere. I never drink anything intoxicating," replied the Protestant.

"Oh, but why not, Yoane? A glass of whiskey is always very exhilarating. You don't know what you are missing," replied the priest taking a big gulp.

A bit later the conniving Priest, blowing a lung-full of smoke into Yoane's face said, "Here, Yoane, have a cigar," proffering him a very aromatic cigar.

"I'm sorry, Monsieur Le Pere, I never smoke."

"Oh, but why not - They are so good. You don't know what you're missing?"

Yoane felt that he had been the target of his teasing long enough. It was time for him to leave. As he said goodbye to guests, the Priest thought that he had been a good sport about the teasing. "Good-bye Yoane" he said, "I'm sorry that you have to leave so early."

"Yes, I'm sorry too, Mon Pere, but I must leave, however, because I must go home to my wife. By the way, Pere, when are you going home to your wife?"

"Oh, Yoane, you know that we Catholics don't believe in marriage for the Priests. We are celibates." "That's too bad, Mon Pere, you don't know what you are missing."

That brought a ringing round of approving applause from all the guests. Many of them had felt the Priest had gone too far in his teasing the Protestant Pastor.

The Priest was put in his place but he was a good enough sport to laugh about it. "O.K., Yoane, you win the final round," was his last remark. ❖

Village Mother on her way to Dispensary

# Yoane Likes Prunes
## Chapter 11

"Missionaries are like Prunes" quipped a certain wag

, "because they go into the interior and do good".

Yoane had never tasted prunes until he was into his sixties, travelling in America. They were strange to him, some being crisp and highly acidulated, while others were wrinkled and crinkled and sweet. Prunes fascinated this preacher.

But the prunes referred to in the analogy were not new to Yoane. With missionary prunes, he had all of his adult life to get acquainted with them. Some were fresh and crisp and attractive, but sometimes too acidulous. Others had too much exposure to the sun. They were dried and wrinkled, and sometimes unattractive. Some were too green, and some too ripe, but like prunes he had seen in the American super market, Yoane had a special liking for Missionary prunes. He loved them — wrinkles, warts, seeds and all. They had come into the interior, and were doing good.

The Richardson family were a package of prunes that he liked very much. When they suffered, he suffered with them. When they laughed, he laughed as heartily as any of them. We have already met Ken, the proper preacher, and Dollie, his adorable wife, and Joyce (Juicy) the beautiful baby.

When Joyce was about eight months old Dollie had a surprise to announce to her husband at the breakfast table. "Ken, I don't know how to tell you this," she muttered through a mouthful of mush, "but I hope you won't be annoyed with me?"

"Annoyed with you! My darling Dollie, how could I ever be annoyed with you? You are my Queen. Why Dollie, you are the apple of my eye, and you are the cream on my pie."

It wasn't often that the proper preacher waxed poetical, but his wife was looking especially attractive. And their lovely baby as beautiful as she was, gurgling in her crib beside the table, how could he resist becoming a bit lyrical?

"But Ken, I'm embarrassed to tell you this. Joyce is just eight months old. She takes a good deal of my time. I should be spending more time with the African women. And now, Ken dear, I think I am pregnant again."

There, it was out. Ken sat there gazing at his wife, thinking how beautiful she was. He was trying so hard to come up with some more poetry that he only heard about half of what his wife had said. While Dollie was waiting, for an explosive response, Ken was dreaming.

However, from the haze of his mind, he seemed to recall several of her words. — Did Dollie say pregnant?

"What! What! - What! Dollie, did you say pregnant? No! You couldn't have! Why Dollie dear, Joyce is only eight months old. It's impossible. I must not have heard you properly. It's that quinine. I'll have to talk to Dr. Kleinschmidt about a hearing aid. By this time Dollie was shaking with laughter. "Yes, Ken, my lover boy you heard correctly. I said 'Pregnant', and that's what I think I am. In fact I'm sure of it, judging from the way I feel."

Dollie suddenly began to look dreadfully pale. She abruptly left the table for the bathroom. She made it in time, but barely. Morning sickness was getting to be a pattern, and how would Ken like this?

"But Dollie, dear", said Ken after she had returned looking as white as a basket of manioc flour, "this is not the way I had planned it, What about the work?"

It seemed that he was stuck on the same broken record that he had played a year and a half ago. He was all for having Dollie reconsider this wild dream. But the more he thought about it, the more he realized that this was in God's hand. No room for manipulating here.

It didn't take long for Ken to get over his objections. "Wonderful. I'm sure the Lord wants her to have a brother (emphasis on the brother). We shall cooperate with him. And it will be a blessed experience for us."

The pregnancy was not all that blessed, with morning sickness and all, but Dorothy pulled it off real well. They dreamed about this one and prayed fervently, as they had for Joyce. The Africans too, were thrilled with the prospect. -

The months sped by. The delivery date was only six weeks away. Ken and Yoane were taking care of the last details preparatory to their trip to the hospital. They were in the church office, arranging for the work when one of the boys came running excitedly, "Oh, Bwana, come quickly. Madame is acting very strangely".

Bwana and Yoane were there on the double. It didn't take them long to see that she was going into labor. - A missionary nurse had arrived several weeks before, just in case of a contingency. She was already boiling water, and setting the stage for the birthday party. She was a young nurse, and this was her first experience with a real live birthday party. - She was scared.

Ken had become proficient in medical work, treating many illnesses successfully. However, in the matter of delivering babies, the only birthday party he had ever attended was his own,some 33 years previously. But the very solicitous father read all the obstetric books and articles he could lay his hands on. He would at least know the theory in case he would ever need to know how.

This was no mere false labor. With Yoane as errand boy, and the nurse at his side as his assistant, Ken was ready. But the poor nurse had never actually witnessed a flesh and blood birth. She was scared. So was Yoane, and when he was not busy boiling water, he was praying.

When the contractions became more intense, and Dorothy let escape a few anxious moans, the nurse fainted into complete oblivion. Not knowing how serious the nurse's condition was, Ken had to neglect his weeping wife, to revive the nurse. After bringing her around he gave all his attention to his very special patient. Coddling, coaxing and even cajoling her into pushing their new little baby out of his pre-natal, comfortable quarters, Ken was doing his best. The obstetrition was preforming well, and so was Dorothy.

Just as Ken had predicted, the little newcomer was a boy. He had long since chosen the name David for his son. With the job of delivering his own son, Pop was exhausted. But he was pleased beyond measure that God had enabled him to stage this party with out a hitch. He immediately sent a cyclist to call for Dr. Kleinschmidt. The doctor's examination revealed that all had been done in a normal manner - all was well.

Yoane was elated that he had assisted the Bwana in performing a safe landing for little David. Both baby and mother were very weak, and David, like Joyce a year and a half before, had a very inadequate supply of milk. A Belgian official happened by, however, and he had his own way of solving that problem, just as he had done for Joyce when she was a little baby. - A hippo-hide whip to blister the bottom of one of the blacks who owned some cows produced an abundant supply. David was on his way, even though he did develop a case of rickets due to a calcium deficiency.

Joyce and David developed well at Adi until it was time to send them to boarding school. - Being British, the parents felt that they should have a British education. They left Adi in 1938 for East Africa to place the children in a British school. In 1942 when we were stationed at Adi the Richardsons came back for a month's visit. Yoane was in a state of euphoria—his old Bwana was coming back.

For Edythe and me their coming was a cause for anxious concern. We had introduced some rather radical changes. For Edythe this was a big worry—how was she ever going to make the kind of tea that would satisfy bibbers of British tea? This could be a potentially embarrassing situation.

Yoane reassured us however, telling Edythe that her tea was very acceptable. And all the changes that had been introduced, hadn't they been discussed with the Church elders, and were we not all of one accord in each of the changes? The Elders would stand with us if there would have to be explanations.

The Richardsons finally arrived. There were acres of black people to welcome them with songs of cheer and noisy greetings. Literally thousands wanted to shake their hands. "Kah! Kah! Kah!"they shouted, "Bino asirayi" (Really! Really! - You have come).

The black reception kept on until dark. Our chance to talk to our guests finally came. Bwana and Madame "Risisi" were not as awesome as we had feared. They were British right down to their British back bones. Their culture was as British as their accent. We two Americans had some learning and adapting to do.

We soon found out that all four of them were very human, and they even appreciated our American jokes. If an American wants to make a Britisher laugh at one of his jokes, he must tell it to him at an early age. By the time he's an old man, he will catch the point and laugh hilariously. But the Richardsons had an appreciation for our stories, and Ken could always match it with a better one, equally understandable to us.

Edythe solved the tea problem by inviting Mrs. Richardson (we would not dare to call them by their first names) to make the tea herself. As to the changes, Ken was not always sure they were for the best, but he was gracious about them. They spent an enjoyable month with us, during which time we developed a friendship that would last to the end of their lives.

Yoane never understood, of course, the prune analogy of missionaries, alluded to at the beginning of this chapter. The strange white creatures walked into his heart long ago, and he always relished them. Another package of prunes arrived, labeled Mort and Esther Steen with two very small prunes, Karen and Raymond, aged 6 and 4. Our son Steve was about 6 months younger than Karen, and 6 months older than Raymond.

Mort and Esther had fallen in love at Bible College. Esther had, as a young girl, accepted the Savior, and she felt that God wanted her to be a missionary. Mort too, as a young man accepted the Savior, and became a student in the same Bible School. Mort was never enamored with missionaries, but he surely was with Esther. The affection was mutual, and when he finally proposed to her, Esther's response was qualified. "Only if you too feel that God is calling you to the Mission."

Mort had to pray over that. That was a hard one. But Esther, as lovely as she was, finally won out. They arrived at Adi, full of glow and glamor. Edythe and I were both well into our forties by then, and we were the only missionaries at Adi until they arrived. The young family brought a surge of new life. They were both ardent linguists, and sunk their talkative teeth with relish into their language lessons. The Kakwas loved them. Mort had an unusual sense of humor.

Yoane took a real interest in the young family. He enjoyed them very much, but he had one concern over Mort. -This new young "mondeli" was very fond of hunting, and Yoane was afraid he was spending too much time hunting buffalo, water buck, elephants and many more. He prayed with us about this, and then he and I decided to counsel with Mort, - who took our advice very well. - It helped a bit, but he still spent a good deal of time in the sport.

After they had been with us for about a year little Raymond came down with a severe attack of malaria. Yoane, along with the whole church, and we missionaries as well, prayed much for the sick boy.

It looked very serious. - After about a week Edythe and I, along with Yoane, met around the little lad's bed. - The parents were sitting on the bed and we prayed earnestly. - Esther was holding the sick boy in her arms as we prayed, and without a struggle, this fine little four year old was translated from his mother's arms into those of his Savior.

Esther sat there bewildered, holding the empty little shell on her lap. Mort was absolutely devastated. Why would God do this? - He wept uncontrollably, repeating again and again, "Why? Why? Yoane was like a tender angel of mercy. He helped the mother lay out the remains on the bed. Then, with arms about the father and the mother, he quoted the most appropriate verses. "Suffer the little children to come unto me. Forbid them not."

And again: "Weep not, for the child is not dead but sleepeth." Verse after passage of verses, he poured on the oil and the wine of the Scriptures over their wounded spirits. Then he prayed so tenderly and with such feeling. — The sorrowing parents responded beautifully to the ministries of this black Pastor who was weeping with them.

Word spread rapidly that Raymond Steen "Asirakei na Lora" (had gone to heaven). The big veranda that reached all the way around the colonial style house was filled with silent mourners. Some finally dried their eyes on their shirt sleeves and began to sing hymns. "There's a Land that is fairer than Day". - all the verses. Next they sang "There is a Happy Land." From one song to the next, singing all the verses.

But plans had to be made for the Burial: likewise the Government doctor, who also acted as medical examiner would want to examine the body. We would have to take the Steen family, along with Raymond's remains to Aba that very night. We kept our Plymouth sedan gassed and serviced just in case of such an emergency. The trip to Aba was about 100 miles.

Raymond's sister, Karen, had gone to bed before Raymond died, as had our boy. We let them sleep until all was in readiness with Mort and Esther seated in the back seat, Mort holding the body of his son wrapped in a blanket. It was near midnight when we finally put Karen and Steve between us and started off. For the two children, between Edythe and me, it was a lark to be going to Aba in the middle of the night. We felt it better to with hold the news of Raymond's death from them until the next day. The two youngsters kept their eyes wide open to see if any wild animals might be spotted in the beam of the headlights. — They were soon fast asleep again for the remainder of the long trip.

We arrived about 4 A.M. Roosters were already lugubriously lauding the new day. There was very little sleep for the Steens, or for ourselves. At about 7 o'clock Karen was at our bed room door, "Oh Stevie," she called excitedly, "Wake up! Just think, Raymond is in heaven and he's playing with Angel children there."

Steve rubbed his eyes and yawned, "Solo" (Really), he responded in the African vernacular. "When can we go see him?"

Heaven was very real to them, and very much more so now, since their little brother was already there. There was no thought of tears or sorrow. Raymond's death to them was a routine matter of going "Home" to a very lovely place with a lovely garden to be with a very lovely Person, Jesus.

Both the parents, and Edythe and I, along with the

Kakwas, took this as a shattering blow. However, it drew us all closer to one another, and especially to the Savior. Esther showed a sterling quality of mature Christian character, exemplifying the all-sufficiency of God's grace. For Mort, however, it was far more difficult. He grew morose at times, and started to think of home in America. This was just too much. Both Yoane and I tried to comfort him, while Edythe and some of the women were a great help to Esther.

One day the bicycle courier brought the mail in from Aru. There was a fat envelope from a Travel Agency, marked for the Steens. We thought this rather strange, but said nothing about it. A few weeks later another envelope came from the same Agent, this time it looked like it might contain passenger ship tickets. We felt that we should confront Mort.

"Yes, Pete, I've had enough of the Mission field. I can't take any more. I'm going home with three goals: 1) I want my old job back, 2) I want to buy a flashy new convertible, and 3) I want to buy my own home."

We shared this news with Yoane, and together we confronted, we counselled and we tried to convince him, "Mort, don't you think that you are acting hastily? Are you sure this is what God wants you to do? - Let's call a moratorium on your plan for a month, for a time of prayer and searching God's will."

It's no use, Pete. I've made up my mind, Pastor Yoane, I'd love to stay on with you. I love the Kakwa people and I love the work. But I can't understand why all of this has had to happen to us."

He and his wife had been tested severely. Neither Yoane nor I could come up with an answer to his question. Nor could we criticize him too harshly. They were a fine young couple. "I know how difficult it will be for you and Edythe, "continued Mort after a puzzled silence." It embarrasses me to leave you with the whole load of directing the Bible School, and superintending the station work. - But I promise you, as soon as I get my old job back, I'll help you financially to carry the work."

With not a few tears from the Steens themselves, and also from Edythe and me, and all the Kakwas, the Steens bid us farewell. They were dearly loved. We did not, however, take Mort's promise too seriously about supporting the work. - After all, he had three priorities that were all contingent on his finding a job. - Too, there was his family to support.

How wrong could we be? - Soon after he arrived in Long Island, New York, a letter came stating that he had secured his old job again and he was on the payroll. "I'm sending a check for $10.00 to the Home Office designated "Adi work fund," he wrote, "and there will be more to follow."

From then on, the Steens included us in their family budget. As regularly as the calendar ticked off the months there was regular support, increasing as his salary increased. That support continued to come all through the years as long as we were missionaries on the field.

A year after the Steens left our furlough was due. The Peter Stams, our co-workers at Adi, had come back from their furlough, so there was nothing to hinder us. When Mort got the news of our coming home, he asked for our arrival date. "I'll meet you at the dock," he wrote." What joy it was to be met by him. He helped us through customs and immigration and led us into the parking lot. He stopped at a sparkling clean and classy convertible. There it is, Pete, that's the baby I used to dream about at Adi." It was beautiful.

He drove us into an attractive residential area, and up to a lovely little home. "There's another one of my goals achieved. My little dream house."

Esther and Karen were there to welcome us, and to show us through their property. Every prospect seemed to please, but there seemed to be something missing.

"Pete and Edythe," Mort said with a sigh, "I've got everything I used to dream about at Adi —and all within a year's time. But I'd give it all up in a moment if only I could get back to Adi.- I feel that I have failed God, and the Adi church. Yoane has been a very choice friend, and I'd like to have a chance to go back and try again. Do you think the Mission will give me another try? Will you intercede for me?"

After our furlough was completed I presented their desire to the Field Council back in Zaire. There was a dubious reaction but they finally agreed that the Steens should have another chance. I sent this news to the Home Council and asked if they could be reinstated. Their reply was a flat "no".

Yoane was broken-hearted about this, as were all of us at Adi. The Steens were disappointed, but applied to another Mission in East Africa. They were accepted and were soon deeply involved in an evangelistic work. They were happy, but Mort was still a bit sad. - He felt that he had failed God at Adi.

By that time I had become Field Director in Zaire and we had moved to Bunia. Mort sent another appeal. In my new official capacity, could I write another letter to the Home Council to please reconsider their request?

It took the H.C. a number of months to answer my letter. When we thought they had ignored it we received a letter from the Home Director. "The Home Council has considered your request regarding the Steens. It is highly improbable to accept such a couple again. However, in view of the unusual circumstances, the Council has gone on record to reconsider them on the proviso that they finish a full term successfully with their present Mission."

But God works in mysterious ways. Shortly after they received the news about returning to Adi, Mort received word from the Kenya Game Warden. There was a rogue-buffalo in the Mombasa area who had killed a number of people. The Game Department must destroy this destroyer. Mort, being an excellent hunter, and also a personal friend of the Game Warden, was asked to help the warden to hunt down this brutalizing bull. Always ready for a hunt, and equally eager to help a friend, the missionary agreed.

The two hunters found the killer and both of them shot him almost simultaneously. Both bullets struck home and inflicted mortal wounds. But the beast was not ready to quit until he had committed one last devastating deed. He charged the hunters and gored Mort. He was seriously wounded, but the warden was able to get him to the hospital at Mombasa. There he was operated on, but he died on the operating table. Yoane was deeply moved over this news. Having a real Pastor's heart, he looked on Mort as a son. He suffered along with Esther over this great loss.

Many missionaries, who are like prunes, came into Yoane's life. — Barriers of class, color or culture were never a problem with him. He loved missionaries like he loved his own blood brothers. He thought prunes were great - wrinkles, seeds, and all. ❖

Banduni with his wife and son

# Under The Belgian Regime
# Chapter 12

The people of the Congo had always treasured their laissez-faire, leisurely life. They had lived under the domain of the spirit-world, and had confidence in their witchdoctor - come flood or fire, famine or fantasy. They felt quite secure with their system of placating the spirit world with sacrifice, either animal or human. They used many devious ways of allaying the anger of the offended evil spirits.

Best of all they had their freedom. They bowed to no one except their own chief or their witch doctor. Life was care free and relaxed.

Then came the invasion of the White man, accompanied with a band of brisk and burly blacks. They cared not about offending the departed spirits, and they killed the venerated chief. They carried strange looking sticks - fire sticks that barked like an offended demon. These sticks spat out fire that destroyed and killed at random. They could kill a buffalo at seventy-five cornstalks away. Older men and women, as well as children of less than twelve dry seasons were killed by these sticks of the devil that spat fire. Teenage children and all young men and women were kept alive, and their legs were tied with chains - short pieces that allowed them to take very short steps as they walked. Groups of these men were chained together and sent far away - across many rivers. The young teenage girls were guarded carefully, and divided among the invaders to satisfy their lustful desires. Villages were burned, and many thousands of children and older men and women were wantonly killed, while the captives in chains were marched out to the great water with the salty taste. There they would be sold to slave traders and put into large houses that floated in the salty sea - never to be seen again.

The Congolese of Yoane's day listened carefully to these stories as they were told by their fathers. They had been passed on from generation to generation. Little children sat around the evening fire, entranced as the older masters of dramatization told with flourish and with hyperbole, the fate of their great-grandfathers.

There was an inbred fear of the white man, but they had not seen any for several generations. Now their freedom meant everything to them. A man wanted, at all costs, to protect his family, and his gardens. He wanted, to order his own life. The demon of slavery was a horror in their minds that they never wanted to return. Their freedom was worth more than life itself. "Live, and let live" was the axiom of their lives. They felt that freedom was their inherent right. Should it be taken away from them by wicked white people? They were sure that those intruders would be banished into a river of molten fire by the spirits.

They learned a proverb: "Never kill a dog on the ground. The earth you walk on will hear the beating of the dog's tail. The earth will remember it. When time is sufficient the earth will curse the killer, and the dog will be avenged."

After these wicked killers, came the Belgians. They were not killers and plunderers as had been the slave runners, but they also struck terror in the hearts of the Africans. They waxed eloquent as they talked about the Belgians.

They took our tree-water (rubber) out of our trees and sent it far away to the big salty water. They came in with huge animals made of iron that uprooted our large mahogany trees like an elephant would push over a little sapling konyuke tree. They tore up our countryside and moved mountains. These iron elephants drank a masanga that the white people called "petrol". It was a firewater that exploded when a burning coal of fire was dropped into it. When they wanted to burn down a village they sprinkled a lot of the fire-masanga on it, and lit one of their little fire sticks that they carried in a little box in their shirt pocket. As quickly as a buffalo can switch its tail the whole village became a roaring flame, fire rushing through the village like an angry simba (lion).

They fished the large white fish which they called Perch out of our lakes and rivers. They took our barter system away from us, and they gave us little round pieces of metal which they call francs. If we want to buy a basket of manioc from our neighbor, we can no longer exchange a rooster for it. Now we must sell the roosters for francs to go and "buy" the manioc with francs which our neighbor uses to buy our rooster with. How confusing. On and on they sit around their fires, spitting at the sparks that leap out from the burning embers. Quite frequently they show enough spitting expertise to quench a burning spark in midair. They begin to get real angry when they talk about the way the Belgians treat their women.

"My third wife is very beautiful" one of the spit-fire conversationalists continues, "and the new Bulamatadi asked her to carry some water for him. As she came up with her beautiful body marching in perfect rhythm under the weight of a seven gallon munungu (earthen pot of water), she set it down in his rest house. He grabbed my wife and threw her on his sleeping mat. He lay with her in the same way that my shenzi dog behaves with the neighbor's dog that is in heat. Had I known what was going on I would have gone in with my spear and killed the dirty nyama (animal)."

Often times the Belgians would bargain with a villager for his daughters and pay the full dowry price. He would go through the native marriage ceremony, meeting all the requirements. Then he would take the young daughter to his own home and live happily with her as husband and wife. He would teach her many things, and dress her with the finest clothes available. The children he raised with his African wife became Belgian citizens, and would receive a proper Belgian education.

With such an arrangement the Africans were well pleased. But to see them come and promiscuously play around with their daughters was repulsive. Taxes became the bane of their existence. They could not understand why the Bulamatadis would take their francs away from them. "What are taxes?" they asked one of the officials.

"Taxes are to be paid for the things the Government gives you, and the many things they do for you. We build bridges for you that are very costly. We build fisheries for you. We send you administrators, policemen and soldiers, all of whom must be paid. All of these are paid for by taxes. You must pay them, or you go to jail."

This was very confusing. The bridges were made from timber that came of forests that belonged to the Congolese. The fish came out of their lakes. The Government functionaires were not at all wanted by the Africans. Why should they pay for things that were profiting the Belgians, and pay for officials they neither needed nor wanted.

"I think I understand," said the chief. "They are like a hunter who had a faithful dog that was a very good hunter. He was also a good watch dog. If an intruder would come to steal chickens at night the dog would chase him away. When the hunter went on safari the dog always was at his heels to protect him.

"But the hunter took very little interest in the dog. He didn't feed him enough. His bones showed through his skin like the skeleton of a calf after the hyenas had their feast. The dog was full of mange and sores. The hunter just did not take care of his dog. "One day the chief met the hunter and the dog. 'Why don't you take care of your dog? He is your faithful servant and your friend, and you treat him worse than your wife. You are an ingrate. If you don't feed your dog properly I will punish you.'"

"Very well, my chief, I hear your words. I will give him a good chunk of meat when I get home."

"That evening the hunter took his dog in his arms. 'You are a very good doggie, and I have not treated you very well. I'm going to give you something very special for supper. I have a very nice piece of meat for you."

With that he put the dog on the ground, and held him between his knees. He took out his very sharp hunting knife and cut the dog's tail off, saying, "Here doggie, here's a nice piece of meat for you. Have a good supper."

"That", concluded the chief, "is the way we understand taxes. Our freedom is being taken away from us, and our tail is being cut off to support this system of slavery."

Yoane was much aware of this attitude, but he was also an astute Bible student. He understands what the Apostle had to say in Romans 13 about the "Powers that be are ordained of God." That it is required of all citizens to pay taxes, and to give honor to those who are in control.

This message he often preached, but during the colonial days it was not a very popular message. Nevertheless Yoane was faithful, and the Kakwa Christians learned that God required it of them to obey the colonial officials. Some of them obeyed with their bodies, and not with their spirits. Like the sheep being dragged by a rope around its neck to the butcher's block.

Belgian policy was very stern. The laws were clearly defined, and harsh. Their justice was quick and sure. But along with harsh justice there was a generous benevolence. A strange mixture of justice and mercy this paternalistic, militaristic, no-nonsense regime that "kept the African in his place".

When a Belgian Official came into the area, the African men were to stand at attention and give him a salute. A person could be flogged for failing to do so. The Official came with pomp and aplomb, often being carried in a tepoy. One that used to come and visit us frequently was of noble birth by the name of Monsieur Noppens. The way the Africans pronounced his name sounded suspiciously like "Monsieur No-Pants." You can imagine what some of our wag missionaries did with that!

Monsieur Noppens was an avid musician, and he loved to play Bach. He always had his violin and stacks of music along on safari. Wearing his broad-brimmed pith helmet (the hat with a veranda, as the natives called it), and his khaki shorts uniform, he was carried in a tepoy. The sun was always too hot for him so he fastened a large sun-umbrella over his portable throne. His violin case was ever at the ready, resting across his knees.

Part of the time he was being carried by four big sweating blacks he was dozing, dreaming about his chalet back in Belgium. When awake he lifted his violin to his chin and played Bach. Perspiration exuded profusely from the pores of his ruddy skin, and the little silk handkerchief, wringing wet, was tucked between his chin and his violin, with eyes closed, absolutely oblivious of the amazed Africans that lined his path to gaze in wonder at the spectacle. He played his classical music.

Invariably when passing through the area Mr. Noppens stopped at our home for a visit, a hot bath and a meal. Not infrequently he would spend the night with us. He was a Flemish speaking Belgian which he preferred to French. This being a dialect of the Dutch language, I was able to visit with him in his own language. He always enjoyed this, and many a time I was able to share with him God's plan of salvation.

The colonial government did have the interests of the Congolese people high on their priority list. The Congo was a wealthy colony for them. So it was of concern to keep the people happy.

They felt that the "natives", as they called the Africans, did not have enough money for themselves. They forced them to plant large cash crops along with the produce they planted for their own consumption. The cash crops included large gardens of peanuts, sesame seeds, and mulberries which the Belgians needed for their silk industry. Crops as these afforded a source of cash income.

Once the government came up with the idea that tobacco would be a profitable crop. Word was sent to all the chiefs that every family should plant several hectares of tobacco. Many of the Kakwas were happy with this prospect of planting a very lucrative crop, and perhaps even becoming wealthy. The elders of the church, however were not at all pleased. They had studied the Scriptures, and were convinced that their bodies were the dwelling place of the Holy Spirit. Was not the use of tobacco harmful to their bodies? Did it not have an adverse effect on their health? How could Christians defile these bodies that were sacred through the use of tobacco?

They began to teach these verses in their sermons. How could Christians have any part in raising a product that was harmful to the body? It wasn't enough merely to abstain from the use of it, but they felt, it was wrong to produce that crop and thus have apart in defiling other bodies. The church made a policy against the planting, and the using of tobacco.

This was in direct opposition to the official Belgian dictum. Such rebellion would be punished by flogging, a heavy fine and a long jail sentence. It was a serious business to defy the Government. Some of the Christians were punished, hoping that their severe punishment would be an example for all the Protestant Christians. But the Belgians did not realize that causing the Christians to suffer for their religious convictions would only make them more determined to do what was right. They counted it all joy to suffer persecution for Christ's sake.

The Belgians were on the horns of a dilemma. They could not allow stubborn Kakwa Christians to get away with such defiance. There would be no end to their rebellion.

On the other hand they could not afford to make martyrs out of them. If they would persecute Christians certainly reports of it would reach the outside world which would be very embarrassing to Belgium. Perhaps they could sweet-talk them into obeying the edict. The Administrator would call a delegation of the church to the chief's village. He would reason with them and entice them to obey.

Yoane led the delegation and he was recognized by the Administrator as the spokesman. He was treated with due respect as they had the discussion under the shade of a mango tree.

"Pastor Yoane" began the Official, "I'm very glad that you and your delegation have come to me to discuss the matter of planting tobacco. You must realize that tobacco is a plant that God has created and it is very good."

He took a cigar from his pocket and showed it to Yoane. He wanted Yoane to take it and smell it, but the Pastor refused to touch it. The Belgian finally lit the cigar and blew a cloud of the aromatic smoke into Yoane's face. "You see, Pastor, it smells very good when you inhale it into your lungs. Try it for yourself."

"No thank you, Mr. Administrator. I do not use tobacco, and I am sure that my Father in heaven does not want me to try it. I see that those who use it become enslaved to it. The cigar becomes a master over them. I know too that many who smoke tobacco soon develop a very bad cough. Many of them die of the breathing sickness."

Yoane continued with respect to give the Administrator the reasons why he himself did not use it, and why the church had adopted a policy of refusing to plant the stuff. The Belgian saw that it would be impossible to change the Pastor's mind. He would try another tactic.

"Very well, Pastor Yoane, I can see that your convictions are firm regarding the use of tobacco. But you don't have to use it. You can preach about it all you want. None of you is forced to use tobacco. All that I'm asking you to do is to plant it and cultivate it so that the Government can buy it. It will be a very profitable crop for you."

"Oh Monsieur, I don't deprive anybody from using or planting tobacco. All I do is to preach God's Word. I read from I Corinthians 3:19 "Know ye not that your body is the dwelling place of the Holy Spirit Who lives in you. You belong to God. You are bought with a price!" There are many other verses that I preach to the church. The Holy Spirit convicts them and they make up their own minds. There they are," waving to the group of Christians,"ask them."

Yoane's unabashed statement rather confounded the white man. He had not expected a homily from this black preacher that would leave him confused and undecided.

"Well, Pastor," he finally responded, "I see that you have studied the Bible well, and that you have your convictions. But you must understand that the Government's only desire is to provide all of the Kakwas with a cash crop that will really help them financially. If the Protestants don't believe in tobacco, they won't have to plant it. All I ask is that they plant some good cash crop from which they can reap good benefits. Couldn't you plant it and then refrain from using it?"

"I'm sorry, Monsieur" countered Yoane, "but Romans 14:21 tells us that "no man should put a stumbling block, or an occasion to fall in his brother's way." In another place we read "It is good neither to eat flesh, nor drink wine, nor anything whereby thy brother might stumble, or be offended." This includes planting tobacco."

More of the Bible! How could he argue with a man who

allowed the Bible to talk for him? This black preacher knew more about that Book than did the priest.

Frustrated, the Belgian asked, "Well, Yoane, if the Protestants don't want to plant tobacco, then how can we help your people earn a bit more money?"

"Oh, Monsieur l'Administrator" responded Yoane readily, "We would be very glad if you could help us with another cash crop. Could you not provide for us a supply of cotton seeds? I'm sure that cotton would grow very well on our land. That would be a crop that we could plant without injuring our conscience."

The Administrator smiled benignly, "We shall have to investigate your suggestion," he said kindly and with deep respect and admiration for this man of God.

The Administrator did send an agronomist through the area to take numerous samples of the soil for laboratory tests to see if,indeed, the ground was suitable for cotton. Not many weeks later tons of cotton seeds were sent to the area. Those who had convictions against the nicotine weed could plant cotton instead.

Yoane was born, apparently with an innate supply of diplomacy. While he did pose a threat to certain officials due to the vast influence and spiritual authority he wielded over the Kakwas, yet he always managed to befriend the officials. One did approach me one time with the idea that both Yoane and Chief Drupa should be sent off to another province. I pointed out to the official that it was far better to have Yoane nearby as a friend and ally, where he could use his influence for the good of the Government, than to send him away and incite the anger of large segments of the Kakwa tribe. He forgot about the idea of deporting Yoane.

The Kakwa Chief, Drupa, was an even bigger jigger under the political toenail of the Belgian Administrator. It seemed that almost every new official assigned to the Kakwa tribe made it a real project to get rid of the Chief. They threatened to blister his royal bottom with a hippo hide whip and the Chief merely responded with a grunt and a grizzly grin. Then he would lean back in his big chief's chair and doze off to sleep. The official knew that if he should lace the blue-blooded black's bottom that he would have a rebellion on his hands.

Chief Drupa came over one day in a gay mood. "Bwana Brashler," he hissed through his alcohol-saturated breath, the Bulamatadis all want to get rid of me. This official is the 19th one that has tried to deport me. Eighteen of them are all gone,and this 19th one too will be gone within weeks. I am still here!"

The Chief and the Belgians were both very important to our work, and Yoane did his diplomatic best to keep up good relations. But the pastor was interested in more than official good will. He wanted to win these "Batu Mokuru" (great people) to a right relationship to the Savior. ❖

Pastor Yisaya Wuli & Yoane Akudri

AKUDRI *143*

# The Leader of The Pack
# Chapter 13

Jesus said, "I will build my Church, and the gates of hades shall not prevail against it". Matthew 16:18

That is what Christ has been doing since Pentecost. The Apostles, in obedience to the Savior's Commission, went every where preaching the Gospel and planting churches. Christ is still building His invisible church by adding the members to it. His followers are still planting and establishing local churches.

The work at Adi is following in the same plan. The Central church grew initially under the leadership of the missionaries. They drew members from the Kakwa district surrounding the Adi station, a radius of about 25 miles. As numbers grew there were more district churches planted, each district having its central church with a presiding elder and several assisting elders. When we arrived at Adi in 1940, there were seven districts.

In those seven districts there is now in each of them a well organized church with an ordained pastor in charge of the entire sub-section. Through out the seven areas there are 21 local churches and 107 local preaching centers. Most of the local churches have either an ordained or licensed pastor. There is a permanent brick chapel with either a metal or tile roof for each subsection church, and likewise in many of the 21 local churches. Yoane has always been regarded as the leader of the pack.

As all great leaders, Yoane was a special target of the devil. He thrived under persecution when it was generated amongst his enemies outside the church. If he were thrown into jail, or hauled into court for trumped up charges brought against him by unbelievers, the effects rolled off him like water from the downy feathers of a duck. With amazing resilience he bounced back into the work without ever taking time off to recover, or to vindicate himself.

But when opposition arose from within the Body, caused by jealousy, or malicious bad-mouthing by some of his peers, it was more than he could stand. Many tears he shed because of avaricious gossip. He was the Lord's choice servant, and the devil was not going to let him get away with his success story without a vicious struggle. However, Yoane was "strong in the Lord, and in the Power of His might". He found that a very effective way of destroying his enemies was to pray for them more diligently, and to love them more dearly. There are still a few who are jealous, but his way of endearing the obdurate is simply to activate the above formula.

He is a great leader. He has the knack of making people miss him while he is away, and following him when he is not. The seven original elders were all very loyal to him. They were: Luka, Rubena, Yeremiah, Yisaya, Abarama, Davidi and Danyele. Several of them have gone to heaven, and have been replaced by competent and consecrated successors.

Yoane has, however, been in great demand as an evangelist and conference speaker, not only widely in his own country, but in surrounding countries of Uganda, Sudan, Tanzania, Kenya and Central African Republic. Consequently, he has been assigned as full-time evangelist. Whenever he comes home to Adi, however, he is still revered as "Pastor".

He has made a tremendous impact on his many preaching peers. One of these is Anderea Banduni who was pastor of a local church for many years. He was of the same family as Idi Amin, the only difference being that Amin was recruited by the devil for devilish designs, while Anderea was recruited by God to do a very godly work.

Like Yoane, Anderea was a great preacher. Many years ago, while Edythe and I were still at Adi, he was called to a conference near the Sudan border. He preached with great unction and the Holy Spirit used him mightily. The conference finished late one afternoon and Anderea tied his safari gear on the back of his bicycle, and started the twenty-five mile trip home to Adi.

On the way he met a herd of elephants rather abruptly. He abandoned his bike, and like a scared chimpanzee, he scaled the nearest large tree. Elephants have very poor sight, but an incredible sense of smell. The gargantuan beasts knew that the preacher was up the tree and they decided to wait, Anderea decided to wait longer. He had more at stake. He waited until dark, and he would wait all through the night if necessary.

Alas! The branch on which he had been very uncomfortably seated decided to break, and the pastor came tumbling down. A sharp piercing pain from his right leg caused him to lose consciousness. The elephants were nearby, but God preserved his servant through the night by miraculously changing the course of the wind. His scent was blown in the opposite direction.

At daylight he had regained consciousness, and he was able to see what had happened. He had sustained a compound fracture of the right tibia. He was very seriously injured, and there was no possible way he could get on to Adi. He was all alone!

Or was he? A verse of Scripture came to mind: "The Eternal God is thy Refuge, and underneath are the everlasting arms" (Deut. 33:27). He committed his predicament to the "everlasting arms".

Only a few moments later he heard voices calling his name. His friends at Adi were expecting him the previous evening. When he didn't show up, they started out to find him very early in the morning in the moonlight. They followed the trail that Anderea should have taken, calling his name as they went. Anderea could hear the voices clearly, and he responded weakly. The rescuers found him very weak and in great pain.

They ministered to his immediate needs, wrapping his leg with the bone protruding out of the flesh in banana leaves, securing it firmly with sapling splints. They made a stretcher of sapling poles and elephant grass, and prayed that God would protect them from the belligerent beasts.

The trip to Adi was extremely difficult for Anderea, but God answered their prayers. Danyele Yeka, the male nurse in charge of the dispensary received the injured patient very solicitously. They had been close friends, and workers together in the Gospel. He did a very clean and efficient job of surgery, setting the bones, and securing them in splints.

However, the wound had been exposed to dust and flies for almost 24 hours. In a few days there were signs of infection. Danyele was frustrated. He must get his patient to the nearest doctor and without delay. The case was critical. He asked the missionaries to take him to Arua, Uganda, where Dr. Williams was in charge of the AIM Hospital.

The Doctor did his best to save the leg, but gangrene had set in. "Anderea", he said to the patient, "I'm afraid I shall have to amputate your leg. If not, the infection will spread through your body and you won't only lose a leg, but you will lose your life."

This was a shocker. "No way, Doctor, will you cut off my leg! I must have that in order to go out and preach the Gospel. You are a famous doctor, and also a Believer in God. You clean and heal my leg, and Yoane and all the folks at Adi will pray. You must save my leg!"

The patient was adamant. No operation that day, and for several more days. Friends and relatives gathered around Anderea's bedside. They read Scriptures and they prayed. But he was getting sicker each day, and his fever crept higher and higher.

Dr. Williams examined his patient again and frowned. "Anderea, you must make a choice. Either you let me amputate your leg or you will be dead within 24 hours. If you let me amputate, I may be able to save your life. If you don't give permission, then I shall start preparing a funeral sermon for you." "It's that bad, is it, Monganga? Malamu (very well), Doctor, start cutting."

The operation was performed that very morning. The preacher was a very sick man, but a successful operation, and efficient nursing care brought him through a severe crisis. With proper diet, he was soon crawling around on the floor.

But he spent hours lying desolate on his bed, reflecting his great losses. No longer would he be able to plant a garden, or to provide for his wife and family. There would be no way of procuring wealth to pay the dowry price for his grown son. Worst of all, he would not be able to get out into the highways and villages to preach to lost Kakwas. Could God have made a mistake? Why should He ever allow this to happen? The once jovial preacher was completely disconsolate.

Anderea had always been a good provider. His gardens were always bigger and better than his neighbors. He could always help others who were destitute. He always had a good supply of chickens from which he could choose a large healthy rooster to give as a gift to Pastor Yoane when he came to his village. He always had a gift for the missionaries. Now he was only a part of a man. His inventory would now be used up to buy food for himself. Now what would he do to find a wife for his son?

Of course, God was still very much alive. Hadn't he often preached glowing sermons on the all-sufficiency of Christ? But now God had let him down. How could he depend on Him now. He had let him down once, He would do it again. All of those beautiful sermons he had preached for others were now abrogated in his own need.

Like Job of old, poor old Anderea sat on the ash heap of his misery, immersed in self-pity. Of course, he still had his old friend and Cousin, Idi Amin, with whom he had grown up. Idi had always owned much personal wealth, and he had always been generous. This would be a source of help.

But as he reflected on his old buddy, Idi, he remembered how he had turned his back on God, the God of the Christians, and embraced Allah, the God of the Islamic faith. In fact, Idi had absolutely no time for Christians. Indeed, he had turned into a monstrous maniac, murdering with impunity thousands of followers of Jesus Christ. Would it be right for Anderea, a strong Christian Pastor, to turn to an enemy of the Gospel for help?

And furthermore, Anderea had always found it more "blessed to give than to receive." His pride would never allow him to become a beggar, and especially, to beg from one who was an enemy of Christ. He sat in utter dejection - despondency - doldrums - defiance. All of these described the attitudes of the disenchanted disciple of Christ.

Seated on his little Kitipala (foot stool) beside his hospital bed, mesmerized in his misery, he spotted a shiny little object, lying on the floor. It seemed to beckon the preacher: "Come, Anderea, look at me. I am yours for the taking".

The preacher was fascinated. What could this be? Getting off his kitipala, onto his one good knee, he nudged himself over to the glittering object. It was a half-shilling coin. "Good Omen", thought he, "No doubt this is from God. It is surely a forerunner of better things to come."

Like Jonah's experience with the gourd - a worm crept in to spoil the refreshing shade. After all, had not Dr. Williams been in his room that morning? Had he not bent over his patient to examine him? Surely, the coin had fallen out of the doctor's shirt pocket. There was nothing to do but give the small sum of money back to the doctor.

Dr. Williams disclaimed the coin. "No, my friend, I did not drop that half-shilling. Certainly the Lord had provided this for you. With that you will be able to buy a chicken."

Elated, Anderea accepted the coin, and guarded it carefully. His wound was healing up nicely. Dr. Williams made him a pair of crutches and helped him to learn to walk on them. Very slowly the preacher developed mobility. When he could leave his hospital room, and get around to see some of his friends his spirits began to rise.

Except for the half-shilling he was still broke. The Saturday market was in full session and Anderea decided to go chicken-shopping. He passed up all the colorful proud roosters for one big hen. A very serious looking bird, and Anderea would, one of these days, have a chicken dinner. He guarded the hen very carefully in his room that first night. In the early morning the cackling creature cackled a cackle that frightened the sleeping pastor out of his dreams. The bird did not want to quit cackling. She had been up to something. Anderea examined the situation, and sure enough - old biddy hen had done her work. A beautiful big brown egg.

He decided not to eat the egg that day because his friends had brought him some food which would do him for a day or two. The process became a daily cackling event that lasted for several weeks. Then abruptly the hen quit cackling, and got down to the serious business of keeping the eggs warm.

In the course of about 3 weeks a dozen lively little chicks pecked their way out of their confining prison shells, and began peeping about their new freedom. The downy little rascals grew as though they were vying for first place in the cooking pot. The preacher was delighted with their antics.

In just a very few months the peepers graduated into the cackling class. Their eggs were not as big as those of the mother hen but they were just as fertile. Result: enough chickens cackling around Anderea's house to sell some of them and buy a lamb.

God was speaking to the preacher that this was His doing. He was taking care of His faithful servant.
Anderea had his broad smile all over his face once again.

Anderea soon discovered that when he bought a lamb he had purchased a pregnant one. Within a short time the ewe lamb got into the reproduction process by producing a set of twins. Then there were three. The baby lambs, not to be outdone by the prolific chickens, in record time they got into the gestation act. The lamb family turned out to be prolific producers. Certainly God had His hand in this because most of the young survived.

The lambs reproduced until Anderea could buy a cow. Not to be out done by the productive poultry or the shaggy sheep, the cow showed signs of gestation. A beautiful calf showed up one morning. Talk about old Jacob being blessed with increased herds, he had nothing over Anderea.

The preacher-turned-farmer and herdsman was very much aware that this was God's doing. "Oh Nzambe," he prayed, "How could I ever become so bitter over losing my leg? I can still get around on my crutches to preach, and the way you have multiplied my flocks and herds have been a testimony of your faithfulness. Please forgive me, Lord, and continue to use me."

The Lord forgave him, and continued to bless him. Dr. Williams was always kind to him, trying to find ways in which he could help him. "Anderea", he said one day, "How would you like it if I would give you another leg?"

"Oh, Monganga", retorted the preacher, "Don't make fun of me. You know that I will always be a "unijambiste" (a one-legger). God has been helping my spirits to feel better in spite of that. But don't try to tease me by telling me that I'm going to have two legs again."

He was irritated that the doctor would make fun of his situation which was still very delicate for him. "But, Anderea, I'm not teasing you. I mean it. I can make another leg for you. Let me show you what I mean."

The doctor proceeded to explain how he would take a limb of a Konyuke tree, which is very light and easy to carve. He would make from it a prosthetic leg. The "unijambiste" was dubious, but he remembered the many incredible things this British doctor had been able to do. "O.K.," responded the pastor, using one of his favorite English expressions, "If you think you can do the work of God by creating a leg for me, I would like to see it."

In a surprisingly few days Williams had carved a facsimile of Anderea's missing limb, one that matched remarkably well the left leg. He had hollowed out the top part of the Konyuke limb, making a deep cup into which the stump of his maimed leg could rest securely. Inside the cup he fitted a thick layer of soft wool which served as a cushion for the stump. What a contraption thought the dubious preacher.

It took a lot of will power and patience on the part of both Doctor and patient. With the use of a cane Anderea began to walk again on two legs. The doctor, and his nurse-wife, Muriel, encouraged him greatly, and did not allow him to quit. Williams promised him a nice surprise as soon as he was able to walk 100 yards without help.

Within 10 gruelling days, before a large applauding audience, he walked the required distance. The crowd went wild in their applause. "O.K., Monganga, I have walked my 100 yards. Now what about the surprise?" The doctor disappeared into his house and soon came back with a package wrapped in newspaper. "Here you are, my friend, the surprise I promised you."

Gingerly and eagerly he tore open the package and brought forth the contents. Anderea was amazed. Never in all his life had he held such a beautiful pair of shoes in his hands, along with a pair of matching woolen socks with no holes in them. The preacher was speechless, and at the point of tears. Dr. Ted helped him put one sock and shoe on his good leg and they fit remarkably well. The Doc himself had big feet too. But how was he going to manage the prosthesis?

Dr. Ted told him to take off the konyuke kicker. He slipped the sock on the wooden leg and stapled it around the top. This worked better than a garter. The shoe was harder to get on, but he finally managed. He laced the shoe and tied the knot securely. "You will never have to remove the shoe and the sock from the leg," assured the Doctor. "Just leave them both as they are, and when you go to bed at night you take off the whole leg."

Anderea was delighted with the Doctors work of art. He wore it all day and at night he hung it on the wall. Never did he worry about getting a jigger in his toe, as he often did with his own foot. But he did take care not to leave it lying on the floor lest the termites begin to grind it to saw dust.

There was only one problem. The leg with the shoe was too nice to wear to the garden. He would certainly ruin the shiny shoes if he wore it for work, or if he walked long distances. But Anderea was ingenious too. He would carve another Konyuke kicker for his work. With the Williams' Wonder as a pattern, he soon had another one for a spare. This he would wear everyday without a shoe, and the other he would use as his preaching leg.

God was really blessing him, and it all started with the half shilling that God had placed on his hospital room floor. He had accumulated enough wealth to buy a wife for his unmarried son. He might be an "unijambiste" but he was still able to care for his family. All of this by simply trusting the Lord, and never once appealing to Idi Amin or to anyone else for help.

But it was awkward for him to get to distant villages to preach. If only he could get a bicycle. Could he ever learn to ride one again with his handicap? Why not give it a try?

If he would sell a cow and a goat he would have enough for a bicycle. He drove a hard bargain on the sale of his animals, and he also prayed earnestly that God would help him to get a brand new one. Yoane was aware of his desire so he also prayed with him. Good BSA British Bicycles were available in the Sudan. One of Anderea's friends agreed to take his money and buy it for him.

It was quite a hassle to get it through customs, and properly registered, but now he had a brand new bicycle that would make him a mobile preacher again. This was God's provision, so he and his friends dedicated it to Him.

Now that he had this bike bronco he had to get a bridle on it and into the saddle. It took a lot of trial and error and patience but he soon had it under control. His phony foot kept slipping off the pedal so he attached a small wooden box on the pedal that formed a nice little cradle for the foot to rest in.

Having the use of his bicycle opened up the whole area to him again. He attached his safari and work leg to the stump of his leg, and fastened his preaching leg, all shod with shoe and sock to the luggage rack. Arriving at his destination he went to the bath house for a soapy splash bath. Then with clean shirt and trousers, he fastened on his preaching leg. The shoe was always shined, as was its mate on the other foot. He looked the part of a country preacher.

Anderea kept thinking of his good fortune. God had certainly spared his life by changing the course of the wind on that fateful night so the elephants couldn't find him. Finally, by bringing him through the infection and serious illness, his spirit was completely revived. Many souls came to the Lord through his ministry. Yoane was as thrilled as Anderea.

Pastor Yoane developed quite a corps of pastors and elders who worked hand in hand with him. They had elders meetings every month, and when we first arrived it had been customary for the missionary to take the chair. Yoane expected me to take full responsibility. That's the way it was done when Bwana Richardson was there, and what mere man would have the audacity to change such a sacred tradition?

"Yoane", I ventured soon after we arrived, "I think we are

making a mistake. All the time you did not have a missionary here you presided very well. Why should you not continue to do so? You know more about the work than I do, and besides, I think it is very proper that a black man should be the top man."

"Wapi, Bwana (Nothing doing, Bwana), You are the white man and you must lead the meetings. You must preach every Sunday and do the baptizing and the marrying and the burying. That is the way we have always done it."

"But Yoane" I protested, "we don't know how much longer the mondeles will be allowed to stay. You must be the leader, and I will stand with you and support you."

This was hard for him to accept, but with prayer and discussion, and finally cajoling, Yoane and I worked out a compromise. I was to preach the Sunday and midweek prayer meetings in Bangala, and he in Kakwa. We would share Communion services together, and also share in the marriages and funerals, with him taking the bigger part of them. Yoane would chair all the business meetings. He was always a very gracious and humble man. He is, however, still the leader of the Pack. ❖

1973 - General Lundalla and Pete

Yoane Akudri at age 85
(a very uncommon age for native Africans to attain)
continues his active preaching circuit by bicycle

## Teaching All Nations
## Chapter 14

"Go ye therefore and teach all nations."

Wherefore? What is the "therefore" there for? It was put there for the purpose reminding the early Apostles that "All Power" was available to them for the purpose teaching all nations the Good News that Christ died for our sins, that He was buried and that He arose on the third day according to the Scriptures (I Cor. 15:2-3).

The Adi church was very sensitive to this Great Commission, and it was their desire to go and teach all nations. The missionary vision was imbued from Jim Bell, the pioneer missionary who started the work in 1922. It was further impressed on their hearts by the words of the Master, "I must work the works of Him that sent me while it is day: for the night cometh when no man can work" (John 9:22).

About 20 years after Jim and Agnes Bell left Adi, Edythe and I were assigned there. We had met the Bells and fell in love with them at first sight. We invited them to come and visit us at Adi. They accepted with alacrity. The Africans were thrilled that the old Bwana was coming back to Adi. They flocked around our veranda by the hundreds to greet them and to bring them gifts. This was that lovely old couple who had brought them the Gospel to Kukalunga. "Kah, Kah!" and "Ghi, Ghi!" were exclaimed again and again as they wrung the wrinkled hands of the pioneer missionaries. The sheer joy of being together again was mutual.

But it would never do to have the old Bwana back "home" without having him preach. That old gold tooth that they had mistaken for brass was still resplendent in Jim's mouth. They not only wanted to hear his sermon preached in Bangala with an American southern accent, but they wanted to see that flashing gold grinder reflect the Gospel from the side of Jim's mouth.

"Yoane", they said to him as he was on his way to his own house, "we want to 'see' Bwana Bell preach again."

"But certainly" replied Yoane, "We all want to see that gold tooth lisping out the Gospel message again."

Yoane came to me, "Could we have a special meeting tomorrow afternoon? We want to hear Bwana Bell preach."

This meeting had not been announced in previous services, nor had there been a bulletin to publish the news of the old "Tata's" (father's) preaching, but the Kakwas had their own system of advertising. They spread the news from hut to hut, and village to village by word of mouth. A real party-line, and very effective.

"Tomorrow afternoon" arrived on schedule, and the brick chapel seating about 500 was filled to the last possible seat long before starting time. They packed in at least 600, and there were about 500 more crowded around the outside of the building, filling the windows and doorways. Bwana Bell, the golden-toothed orator, would flash his dental decor once again, and nobody wanted to miss this. The Bells were delighted with the enthusiastic crowd. Jim was not aware of the golden attraction that was in his mouth, but he was thrilled that they had come to "hear" him. The size of the crowd humbled him, as did the warm response.

The year this took place was 1942. There were about eight trumpeters to help the congregational singing. Yoane led the singing, and loud was beautiful. They would show the Bells how "beautifully" they could sing.

Then Yakobo Ata, the head school teacher, led the congregation right into the courts of heaven with his prayer. His face was aglow, and his gestures majestic as he ascribed "glory and majesty and power to Him that sitteth on the Throne". The tone of the meeting was set by Yakobo's prayer.

Jim began to preach. He was a bit over come with emotion as he saw Yoane Akudri, Danyele Yeka, Yakobo Ata, Yerimia Banga, Rubena Yisa, Yisaya Wuli, Luka Araba - all of the old elders sitting in their places. There were scores and scores of black faces that the Bells remembered. Jim's thoughts went back to the beginning of the work when these black leaders were youths in loin cloths. Many of the church leaders, for want of a piece of cloth, had then come in their skin suits. Now they wore Khaki shorts and shirts. Some even wore shoes.

Jim's heart flowed over as he began to preach. "And other sheep have I which are not of this fold; them also I must bring" (John 10:16). He praised God for the Adi fold, and the family of sheep. There had been a remarkable response to the preaching of the Gospel, and the growth was great.

"But my dear sons and daughters, do you realize that there are many many tribes around you here in this part of Africa that have never heard about the Good Shepherd. They are lost sheep, not of this fold. Remember what the Savior said, "Them also I must bring".

The gold tooth flashed in a delightful dazzle, but his congregation forgot all about that. They were now engrossed in the content of his message. Those "other sheep" in this case were the pygmies of the Ituri forest, about 400 miles to the southwest of them.

In his message he told how they had left Adi to begin a work amongst the pygmies. There were some that responded, and a few small churches had been established, but the majority of them were still lost sheep, under the spell of the witch doctor and his witchcraft.

The message was a wet one. It was delivered through tears that coursed down his sun-tanned and tarnished cheeks. More moisture oozed through the pores of his entire skin. It was hot in the crowded chapel, and also, Jim was warmed up to his subject. Pygmies were dying without Christ, and only a very few were concerned about them. Would God touch the hearts of some of these to join him in the "Battle for Truth" among the pygmies?

The service started at 2 o'clock and it was near 5 when he sat down. There was a hush over the vast audience. The Kakwas had never seen Pygmies but they had heard about the race of peewee people in the huge forest. Many Africans, and Belgians as well, said that the pygmies were not real people - just another family of monkeys. But here Bwana Bell was weeping over them. He said they would perish without Christ unless we were obedient to the Great Commission. God was touching their hearts.

Yoane arose to close the meeting with prayer. No more singing. Nothing to sing about now after they had seen their beloved Bwana weep over a lost pygmy race of people. Yoane was very subdued as he led in the closing prayer. What would God have him to do? The entire congregation was deeply touched.

The Bells stayed for several days after that historic meeting. But, as all good things must come to an end, so did this visit. A large group gathered around their car as they prepared to leave. Yoane, the leader of the pack, led the crowd in a prayer for safe-keeping of the Bells. He also included petitions for the pygmies: "Oh, Nzambe, show us what you want us to do about the lost condition of our little brothers and sisters".

About a week after the visitors left there was a "hodi" (african doorbell) at the door. There were two fine leaders, both of them school teachers, and both preachers. Edythe and I had talked about these very men, that they would seem as good prospects for the job in the Ituri Forest. In fact, we had prayed about them.

They were Yonatana Wai, and Yisaya Buki, and they took chairs we offered them. They sipped leisurely the tea that Edythe set before them. They were in no hurry and talked about many things. Both were very jovial.

"Bwana and Madame Bell are doing a great work in the forest," Yisaya finally said, coming to the purpose of his visit. "We believe they need some help."

"Bwana," continued Yonatana, "We have both prayed much about this, and God has laid it on our hearts to offer ourselves, and our families, to go to the forest and be missionaries along with our Tata and Mama."

"Praise God," Edythe and I both exclaimed. That is exactly what we have been praying about. God is answering. But, have you discussed this with your wives? Are they with you in this?"

"And why should they not be?" retorted Yisaya. "Didn't we pay the dowries for them? Are they not supposed to do as we tell them?"

"Yes indeed" I replied, "you are the heads of your home, and your wives are to be submissive. But when God calls a missionary, He also calls his wife. You must go and pray with them, and decide this matter with them. Further more, have you really considered what it will cost you to be missionaries in the forest? The food will be different; the climate damp and humid; there will be much sickness. The people will steal from your gardens."

The two men listened politely, but it was clear to see that they were not in the least impressed with our precautionary remarks. "Bwana," interjected Yisaya, "there will be no problem about our wives. They know about our desire, but we will pray and discuss with them as you suggest. But isn't this exactly what Bwana Bell was talking about. He needs us. Let me ask you a question. When Jesus was with the Father in glory, and He saw our need here on earth, did He ask what kind of a climate He would find, or what kind of food He would eat, or whether the people would receive Him? Absolutely not! He asked no questions but He came voluntarily, leaving all of His wealth and glory in heaven. He came and died for us. Isn't it true, Bwana, that the Bible says, "Let this mind be in you which was also in Christ Jesus Who became a servant for us, and died for us?" We feel that God is calling us and wants us to go. Will you take us?"

What can one say in the face of such reasoning and questioning? "Of course I will take you," I answered. "When can you be ready to go?"

Our little old 1934 Ford Pickup was not too road-worthy. It took us several days of repairing and servicing to get it ready for the 400 mile trip through the forest. No tarmac except for the one mile that ran through the center of Bunia. The remaining 399 miles was dirt road with lots of pot holes, and turned very muddy at the first signs of rain. But God was in this, and He would see us through.

Within several days we were ready. There were 8 children and 4 adults piled in the back. Baskets of food; two bicycles tied on the sides; a dozen or more chickens trussed up; a few items of extra clothing; their song-books and Bibles; bows and, a good supply of arrows and spears. There was also a sling shot for each of the boys. That was the extent of their outfit, -a far cry from the tons of supplies and goods that go into a modern American missionary's outfit.

But this was all they owned, and we managed to get the outfit and the 12 bodies into the back of the pickup. Yoane got into the front seat with us. The load was far too heavy for the little vehicle, but Deut. 33:27 was our safari verse, "The Eternal God is thy Refuge, and underneath are the everlasting arms".

On the trip we had a generous supply of flat tires, fuel pump problems, boiling radiators, and several spring problems. God helped us in every difficulty. In less than a week we arrived safely at Oicha, in the heart of the Ituri Forest, the home of the Pygmies.

Jim and Agnes Bell were over joyed to see us. This is what they had been praying for, and when the black missionaries arrived it seemed too good to be true. We stayed with the Bells about a about a week, giving Yoane and us time to go on several short safaris among the little forest people. We found them very friendly, and overjoyed with the idea that two families of giant Africans were going to live with the Pygmies.

Yonatana and Yisaya would settle in a large pygmy center about 25 miles away from Oicha, and that distance from the nearest motor road. Their's would be a life of sacrifice, but both families were ready for their new pioneer life, far out of reach of any semblance of civilization.

The story of their work and life with the pygmies has been told in my previous book, CHANGE. Both families spent over 25 years in the forest. The pygmies soon learned to love them, and regarded them as their parents. The pygmies began to respond to their preaching and a nucleus of Pygmy Believers was established.

The black missionaries not only learned Swahili, which pygmies spoke all through the forest, but they also learned a couple of their tribal languages. They established elementary schools, and soon the pygmies were reading and writing Swahili. The Belgian officials were amazed. How could these little "nyamas" (animals) ever learn to read and write? But the little forest people were quick to learn.

The Believers studied the Catechism book, and memorized it. After being examined by the church elders from

Oicha they were baptized and formed into local churches. Some of the bright young men were sent to Oicha to enroll in the Bible School. After graduating they became pastors, under the supervision of Yisaya and Yonatana. Today there are many well organized and thriving pygmy churches, and some of them are pastored by ordained pygmy pastors.

After only two years in the forest, Yonatana lost his beautiful wife in childbirth. Both of the men lost a number of children to the ravages of the forest. Sacrifices such as these caused them to be closely identified with the pygmies. They were missionaries in the true sense of the word, just as much as any white missionary that ever went from America or Europe.

The Adi Church had become a missionary "sending church". They undertook the total financial support of these families, and continued to support them as long as they continued their missionary job.

Not only did they send missionaries to the pygmy forest, but also to the Sudan, another country altogether. Yoane also went on extended missionary journeys into the Uganda tea fields. Many thousands of people, representing numerous tribes from Uganda, Congo, Tanzania and the Sudan were settled in large heterogeneous villages. The men worked in the tea plantations by day, and raised iniquitous pandemonium by night. What a phenomenal missionary opportunity. With this missionary endeavor, there was soon a Christian Church established. Yoane was invited back again and again. He made the 300 mile trip on his bicycle, taking about a week on the road. He would spend a month or 6 weeks preaching several times every day in chapels and in the market places. "Teaching all Nations" was the theme of his life.

The town of Watsa, an important mining center in the Northeast Congo, was another fertile field for Missions. Thousands of heterogeneous tribes were settled in this town to work the Government gold mines. Watsa was in the Aba district, and the responsibility of the Aba Church. However, the need for evangelists and teachers was great, and Adi responded to this need. Four families volunteered for this work, and for over 30 years they spent their lives faithfully serving the Lord in the Watsa area.

One of these was a bright young man named Tadayo. He had learned to play a trumpet and a trombone, and he was a good song leader. He was a joy to be with, being of such a radiant disposition.

One day when Tadayo was a young man, Dr. Kleinschmidt and his nurse/wife, Coralee visited the Adi Dispensary. Tadayo had been sick so he was in line for an examination. Some suspicious blotches were discovered on his chest that caused the doctor concern.

"How long have you had these spots, Tadayo?"

"Oh, they have been there for about six moons," answered Tadayo. "They are no problem. They never hurt."

The doctor probed a bit, and surreptitiously pierced the skin with a needle. There was no pain response, and this confirmed the doctor's suspicions. He followed this with some laboratory tests which came back with the report: "positive - Hanson's Disease". This simply meant that Tadayo was a leprosy patient.

We visited him in his hut when we heard this news. We found him sitting on his "kitipala" (stool). His shenzi dog lay at his feet, looking as dejected as did his master. His hair was unkempt, and his dirty shirt tattered and torn. Instead of wearing his khaki shorts, he had a blanket wrapped around his loins - a sure sign of a sick person. Flies were flourishing, and he made no attempt to swish them away. "Well, Tadayo," I began weakly, "You look like your favorite goat has died. Do you want to tell me about it?"

"I've got Kebukebu," he grumbled, not bothering to look up to us. "Now I will never be able to preach anymore. I will be isolated in the leper colony. Nobody will come to see me. Why doesn't God take me home?"

We had no answer for his question. "But, Tadayo, there is a real possibility that your disease can be treated with a new drug, and that your leprosy will go to sleep in your body."

I explained how Dr. Kleinschmidt had told us about the miraculous success they were having in treating "kebukebu" with a sulfatron drug. "He wants us to take you, and another young man that has the disease to Aba to start treatment. You will be the very first patients in this whole area to receive this medicine. It might take a year to treat it, and a cure cannot be guaranteed, but there is a possibility that the disease will go to sleep in your body."

The other young fellow was Danyele Amange. We explained to them both as best as we could about the drug, and about the possibility of the disease going into remission. They were both keen to be the first guinea pigs to try the treatment.

We took them forthwith to Aba. The treatment began to have an immediate and dramatic effect on the disease. Within weeks the spots began to clear up, and the symptoms of kebukebu were disappearing. They both wanted to get back to Adi, and get back to their work. "Impossible!" replied the Doctor, "You must remain here under treatment and observation for at least a year. I want to keep a close watch on you."

This was a disappointment to the young men, but their relish for life and activity would not allow them to become remorseful again. Tadayo had his trombone, and he kept busy everyday at the Chapel services. He not only played his instrument, but he preached. His alluring charm, plus his zeal for the Lord, made him a favorite among the patients. Many of them were attracted to the Savior through his ministry. He also taught classes in music. If he was to be at the hospital for a year, he wanted it to be busy.

Danyele Amange was of quieter disposition - more studious. His medical treatment intrigued him. He wanted to learn all that the doctor knew about medicine. He watched the doctor perform operations and Coralee dispense medicines. He was Coralee's favorite and she taught him many things.

"Danyele," she said one day, "if you must be here for a whole year or more, why don't you enroll in the para-medic course? There you can learn what sickness and medicine are all about."

"Solo, Madame (really, Madame), would it be possible?"

It would, and it was. All the while he remained under

treatment he faithfully followed his medical course. In fact he stayed after his treatment for another four years to become a qualified paramedic, with a certificate of graduation. He also passed a government exam, given by a jury of about 10 qualified medical persons. With this certificate he was qualified to direct a rural dispensary and to diagnose and prescribe treatment. He was also able to perform minor surgery.

He was assigned to the Adi Dispensary to work under the capable and faithful Danyele Yeka. After some twelve years of this partnership the latter Danyele died, and Danyele Amange took over the directorship of the dispensary.

Tadayo went home to Adi after his leprosy went into remission. For several years he continued his treatment, and under went a doctor's examination every six months. Even today - 35 years after the disease was detected, the doctors do not consider him as a cured leprosy patient, but rather, an "arrested case".

As a young man, Tadayo lost his first wife, and he was left with several small children. This devastated him, and he mourned greatly his loss. He seemed to lose his zest for living.

But weeping, while therapeutic for the soul, could not go on indefinitely. He was now both father and mother to his children,and life must go on. He had to provide for his family.

Several years passed and Tadayo was still a single parent. "Tadayo," we suggested, "don't you think it's time that you start praying for a wife. You need a help-mate, and your children need a mother."

"Oh, Bwana," he giggled, "I'm getting along fine. And besides, I don't have time to go shopping for a wife. And worse than that, I don't have the money to pay for one. For me to find enough wealth for a dowry, I would have to leave my children and go to work in Uganda for a year. I would have to leave my children with my pagan family to care for them, and they would become real 'bashenzi' (raw pagans) during that time."

He giggled a bit more. The thought of a wife seemed

appealing. But he sobered, "No, Bwana, I believe God wants me to care for my children. And if the Catholic Priests can perform their ministry in a life of celibacy then I can do it too."

"Well, I think you ought to at least pray about it," argued Edythe.

"With a shrug and another giggle he dismissed our suggestion, wondering if we weren't bordering on meddling just a little. But the seeds of connubial complacency had been sown in his young heart. "No doubt," he dreamed, "it would be nice to share my life with a consecrated companion again".

Months later we received a letter from him. "I have followed your suggestion," he scrawled, "I have begun to pray about a wife. Not only have I prayed, but I have tossed my eyes over into the female section of the church, and there is a young girl there who pleases me very much. I would like to ask her to marry me, but the dowry problem is still the same. If only the Lord would provide me a cow, it would encourage me to believe that this is God's plan for me, and that in due time He will provide the full dowry. Will you pray about this?"

Edythe still has a touch of romance about her, and surely we would pray earnestly about this. But wasn't there something more we could do to help cupid along? After my years with this romantic woman I could just see wheels of romantic intrigue spinning. I could almost guess what it was.

We both believed that God was beginning to answer our prayer by setting Tadayo to praying about it, and to looking for some sign of encouragement. Edythe was not just going to let this pass without doing something about it. I surmised that she had designs on my check book. When she had that glittering gleam in her eye, I knew there was nothing I could do about it.

"O.K., my Love, I think I know what you're up to. You want to be cupid's companion in a plot, don't you? And I know too how utterly impossible it is for me to be pragmatic when you get a preposterous idea in your head. You want to buy a cow for Tadayo, don't you?"

"Well, maybe just a little cow," she coyly confessed. "How much money do we have in our account?" It was useless to argue, and I had to admit that it was a pretty good idea. We examined our pecuniary resources, and got a check into Tadayo's hands forthwith. He had his first cow, and not just a "little" one like Edythe had first suggested when she was trying to sell me on the idea. Having made her point, she now insisted on a "big cow," "One that is nursing her baby calf, that would grow into a hefty heifer. That would count for two cows, wouldn't it?"

Cupid's helper had the dowry on the way. Tadayo was exuberantly happy with his cow/calf addition. He had certainly not expected this. He had asked for our prayers, but he did not think we would help God answer our own prayer.

From then on Tadayo got into the act seriously. He made a trip to his brother's village to see if they could help. "Surely, we will help you as best we can. After all, we don't want you to live and die as a bachelor."

Tadayo also sold some personal effects. Soon he had enough to pay the bride price. Her name was Perepetoa and she was beautiful. When he asked her to marry him he discovered too that she had cast wistful eyes in his direction.

We were invited to their mud-wattle house after they were married, and she had it fixed beautifully. She fit into her new role as mother, housekeeper and bride beautifully.

"You know, Bwana and Madame, when I started praying for a 'bibi' (wife) I asked God to give me one who first of all had a 'moyo na maradadi', and that the 'mwili na maradadi' was not important (who had a beautiful heart rather than a beautiful body)."

His wife was sitting shyly by as he said this, trying her best to blush, but her beautiful ebony colored skin would not cooperate. Actually, Tadayo's prayer was abundantly answered. He did marry a young woman with a beautiful heart. But the "exceeding abundantly above" was that God threw in a beautiful body as a fringe benefit. He had thought he would never be happy again with another woman, but how wrong could he be?  He took Perepetoa and his children to Watsa where they continued as missionaries to the miners for many years.  Just recently, after many years of blissful marriage, Perepetoa died.  Tadayo is once again a bachelor, and an old man - still exuberant in the Lord, but looking forward now to a reunion in heaven. ❖

Left to right Pastor Balonge, Pastor Yoane Akudri
and Church President, Etsea, in Zaire

## In This Free Land
## Chapter 15

It was the Fourth of July, 1970, in Bunia - our fifth consecutive Independence Day in this newly Independent country -away from our own Free Land. There was to be no parade and no American flag waving over this newly-freed Land of Zaire. Everything was so different than in our "Land of the Free and Home of the Brave". Fireworks or watermelon picnics would not set this day off as a special one. It was life as usual.

Any sign of American patriotism would be a sure ticket to the "bloc" (prison), where one could be incarcerated for weeks before anyone would bother to inquire why. We had a large American flag, given to us by the American Ambassador, but we had been told to keep it out of sight. My prized little tie clasp with an emblem of the American flag was not to be worn in Bunia. The Zairian Government was "Pro-American", but with an ulterior motive of getting American aid.

So here we were, Ambassadors for our Lord, but a bit homesick for a good old fashioned Fourth of July celebration. We could identify with Mary-Lee Demarests' Scottish hymn:

"I'm far frae hame, an' I'm weary Aften whiles;
For the longed-for hame-bringin,
and my Father's welcome smiles."

The Congolese had developed this Xeno-phobic spirit because of the Belgians during their colonial days. The Zairians, as they were now called, knew well the history of their own country, how in 1885 King Leopold II of Belgium had gained control of the vast Congo Basin - 910,000 square miles. The king regarded himself as an enormous feudal lord, and the whole Congo was his land to let out to his Belgian vassals as he capriciously chose. The natives of Congo were regarded as slaves, and treated with sadistic savagery. The country, rich in natural and mineral resources, made the Belgians wealthy by exploiting their slaves, the legitimate owners of the land. Talk about a "Happy Hunting Ground", this was it.

The unspeakable cruelty and heinous treatment to which the Congolese were subjected was not forgotten. The record of this was not written in the annals of history, but they were written indelibly in their minds and hearts, and passed on from generation to generation. No wonder their attitude toward the white man became misanthropical.

Belgium's cruel treatment of the Congolese was not hidden from the eyes of the world. Europe and America were outraged at such atrocities. Pressure was brought on Belgium, and in 1908 King Leopold was forced to create the "Congo Free State". This developed into the Belgian Congo as we knew it until 1960.

The Colonial Administration became a Potpourri of benevolence and brutality. Their paternalistic care resulted in a measure of medical care and public health. They created good graded roads throughout the colony, and offered good police protection. Veterinary service was introduced, and an Agricultural program with schemes to upgrade their herds and their flocks. The cruelties of the witch doctor were brought under control.

Brutality was evidenced in the way they administered swift and cruel justice. Their prisons were unspeakably horrible. The cruel hippo lash was given for the slightest infractions. Should one dare not to remove his hat, or to stand in the presence of a Belgian, he could certainly count on cutting lashes across his bare buttocks. Punishment in those times was cruel and unusual.

In the 1950's many African countries had their fill of paternalism and Colonialism. The Swahili word "UHURU" (Freedom) became the continent-wide slogan. They were no different from us, in America, some two centuries earlier. "Freedom" and "Revolution" were the cries of their beloved country. Most of the African nations won their independence during those years.

But Belgium was not ready to give their colony Independence. They did realize, however, that a change must come. They must placate the Africans by giving them a voice in their local government. Yoane and I were both invited to attend the meetings of the territorial council that met at Kumuru each month. There was also a Belgian priest and a Congolese Priest, as well as Chief Drupa and one of his assistants.

This was like throwing a meat ball to a wolf. They bolted it down, but it was too little too late. Nothing would satisfy the Congolese now but total Independence, and the complete removal of all Belgian Control. They wanted it instantly. In the early days of 1960 a climax was reached. Riots and bloodshed were breaking throughout the colony. The Belgians were terrified and many of them left the country, abandoning their plantations and businesses.

The new young King Baudouin arose to the occasion. He came to Leopoldville (now Kinshasa) and met with the radicals. There was to be no option - Independence, or total destruction. The King saw that it was useless to try to compromise, and futile to take up arms and fight. He acceded to their requests and promised them full independence by June 30th, only 4 months away.

The Congolese flew into a wild state of euphoria. They took no note of the fact that they would be totally unprepared to govern themselves, nor did they count the cost involved. They wanted independence at all costs. Life was hectic during those months.

Nobody seemed to know actually what Independence was. It was reported to us that some of our friends went to the Belgian Administrator with a large basket, demanding their share of independence on the spot. To explain the abstract concept to people who thought only in concrete terms was most difficult. But Independence was a magic word that must surely mean a panacea for all their social and political ailments.

June 30th finally arrived. Our furlough was unwinding and we were trying to get finances for our return. The transition from a colony to Independence would be peaceable, we were led to believe, and our work would go on as usual. News coming to the States by the Press, however, was different. There were reports of rioting and bloodshed. Belgians and other whites, were beginning to evacuate. This caused our supporting churches to have misgivings about our return, making it difficult to generate both financial and moral support.

But Yoane was appealing for us to come back as soon as possible. It was not until the end of 1960 that we had money in hand. We had prayed much, but it was not without trepidation that we left in November of 1960.

We sailed from New York on the S.S. Statendom, arriving in Southampton on a bitterly cold day. The London news boys were hawking their papers, "Riots in the Congo!" "Whites being murdered!" Such headlines made us want to go back to the State of Washington.

But we were assured by God. "When He putteth forth His own sheep, He goeth before." And "Go ye — and lo, I am with you always." We were not brave. We were scared - all three of us. Yet God was sending us, and we would try to go courageously.

We arrived in Congo soon after Christmas. Steve was to go to Boarding School at Rethy. It was like wrenching a right arm and leg from us to leave our seven-year-old at Rethy, and putting 200 miles of treacherous terrain between us. Steve was a trojan about it, and we toughed out our tears until we were out of his sight. Then we stopped the car and wept bitterly, experiencing what so many missionaries are willing to face for the Gospel's sake. The Stams drove us back to Adi. It had been six months since Independence Day - just long enough to show us what devastation could be wrought by a swashbuckling array that was in full control. There were burned out hulls of automobiles along the road - cars that had once belonged to the proud Belgians. The trip was hot and dusty. It was good to get back to Adi, but Adi, too looked dismal.

Yoane and all the Kakwas met us with open arms. Independence was in vogue, but the people were disenchanted. They had had their fill of colonial cruelty, but what they had thought would be a peaceful transition turned out to be a nightmare.

"I was ashamed," said Yoane, "of the way our Congolese people behaved toward the colonists who really wanted to help us get started. Greedy, soldiers came from Kinshasa and moved into the Administrative offices. They burned the files and important documents. They moved into Belgian houses before they could remove their personal belongings. Our people became more cruel than the Belgians had ever been. They certainly did not behave as Christ taught us." Yoane was ashamed.

We sympathized with them, but what could we say. There were always spies around to report whatever we would say. About the only thing we could say was "Tiens! Tiens", the equivalent of "Well! Well!" - This was a handy little innocuous expression that could say a lot, but never really get us into trouble.

"You know, Yoane", we finally said, "when our country got their independence from England there was a lot of "fujo" (confused mess) there too. It took many decades to bring our country into a peaceful and prosperous economy. It was only the prayers of the faithful that helped us survive."

"Yes, Yes, but you also had your George Washington, your Benjamin Franklin, and your Thomas Jefferson," replied the head school teacher. "They were strong God-fearing men that started your country. What can we do to make our beloved Congo into a strong nation of Africa?"

"The Bible teaches us to be good citizens", we offered, "and that we should pray for and honor our leaders. The only hope for this country is prayer. God will answer, and He will raise up strong men of faith to lay the foundations for your country, and lead you in paths of righteousness."

The elders with Yoane were a bit dubious. "We have been praying, Bwana, and we shall continue to do so. But now you are back and we have planned a big conference. We've got preaching for you and Bwana Stam to do, and there will be many unsaved Kakwas and Lugbaras here."

There were 4000 people present for the Friday and Saturday services, and about 5000 on Sunday. Each day started at 6 A.M. with the large chapel crowded for a prayer meeting.

By 9 A.M. the chapel was crowded to capacity with several thousand seated around the outside. The services ran through until noon without a break. After lunch and a short siesta the crowd was bigger than ever at 2 P.M., and the service continued until dark.

It was great to share in the preaching again after being out of the country for over a year. The Bangala language came back freely, and God blessed all the speakers. Many souls were saved during the conference, and life was good. It seemed like a little vacation from the country's confusion, on the island of Paradise. We forgot momentarily about Independence and political pandemonium.

But the little period of utopia didn't last. The church members dispersed on Monday after the conference, and reports of fighting in all the large cities began to filter through. Lumumba, the country's first premier, had been killed. The whole nation was thrown into turmoil. The whites that were still in the country were being made scapegoats, and many of them were arrested and some were killed.

Word came to us at Adi by radio transmission that we must evacuate into Uganda as soon as possible. By Wednesday, after the conference, we were ready to go. We left all the furniture and personal belongings of the three missionary households in their places. "Don't worry", said Yoane. "I will take care of your houses personally, and will be responsible for keeping them well guarded." For several months he slept each night in the missionaries houses, rotating from one to the other.

A large crowd gathered around our cars to bid us farewell. Many sobbed unabashedly. Yoane prayed: "Oh, Nzambe!" - He halted for a few seconds to put a leash on his emotions. Then he continued his prayer that God would not only keep us safely, but that we would soon be able to return.

In the noonday heat we started our trip - a hot and dusty one. We were stopped by soldiers three times during the 50 mile trip to Aru, the border town. The soldiers were gruff with us, and searched our cars and ourselves. Thank God, no one was hurt.

At Aru we stopped at the Immigration office to get our "Laisser Passer" (permits to leave the country). Instead of getting the precious magic documents we were all arrested. We were three car loads of missionaries, and we were kept under guard in the military camp.

We were hot and thirsty, but there was no water to slake our thirst, or to wash our faces. We could not get to our cars for our drinking flasks. Life was awkward. We sat in a circle - some on the ground, and there were a few uncomfortable chairs for the women. At six o'clock the sun began to sink into the western horizon like a big beautiful red ball of fire. The cool evening breeze began to circulate, and to blow the heat waves away. Our thirst was not to be assuaged.

We tried our diplomatic best to talk our way out of the camp and through the border. Absolute futility to talk to these blackguard, booze-bibbing, brigand soldiers. Finally, near midnight, a captain came into the camp. He joined us in our circle.

"What are you mondelis (white people) trying to do? I see you want to run away into Uganda to try to contact the Belgians so they will come back and rule our country again. But forget it. You are under arrest, and you will have to wait until the Colonel comes from Bunia to decide what he will do with you. He may want to shoot you all right here, or he may want to take you to Bunia to put you in prison."

Certainly not very encouraging. "But Mon Cher Capitaine" we answered, "you can't keep us here like this. We need water and food. Surely, you are not going to be as mean to us as the Belgians were to you. You, Congolese, are good people. We have worked with you for 20 years, and we know that this is not Congo custom to treat visitors from a far country in this way."

"Yes" agreed the Captain, "We, Congomanis, are good people. We love you white people. By the way, if you will give me a quart of whiskey out of your car, I think I could arrange for your "laisser-passer" to get you to Uganda."

We could not bribe our way out for two reasons: 1) we did not have the bottle of hooch, and 2), we had scruples against using bribery. We would have to try something else.

As we talked, we had a good opportunity to present the Gospel to him. "But I don't need that," objected the Captain. "Am I not already a Christian? Haven't I already been baptized? Don't I go to church every Sunday?"

The Captain began to yawn. "I am going to bed", he said. "I have a beautiful soft bed that is very comfortable. It used to belong to the Belgian Administrator. I have a very pretty little slave girl already in bed, waiting for me. Bon Nuit!"

"But what about us?" we objected. "You say you are a Christian. Would a Christian leave Christian missionaries out here in the open all night? Would he leave them hungry and thirsty? What kind of Christian are you?" we persisted.

"Oh, I had forgotten that you might be thirsty. I'll send for some water."

The water was tepid and rancid, but so good! As we drank he smiled benevolently. Wasn't he the kind of person that Christ had spoken about - giving a cup of "cold" water. He was pleased with himself.

"I'm such a good Christian," he crooned through his booze-befuddled breath, "I am going to release you. But you cannot go to Uganda. You must all go back to Adi and stay there to work for the Congolese. You will be good hewers of wood and haulers of water. Go back to your station, and don't try to sneak across the borders. There are soldiers on patrol all along the frontier, and they will shoot you on sight if they see you near the border. If you do as we tell you, we will let you stay alive."

It was a long dismal dusty trip back to Adi. We arrived as the cocks of the morning were crowing out their cacophonous chorus. At least they had something to crow about.

As the three cars rolled up the Africans were jolted out of their sleep. They didn't believe their eyes. Since we had not returned the evening before, they were sure that we were safely in Uganda. They were relieved to see us alive, but alarmed that we had not crossed the border.

They began immediately to prepare a long, over-do break-fast, with pots of steaming tea. The Richardsons had taught them long ago that there was nothing like a cup of piping hot, well brewed tea to alleviate one's thirst. Four or five cups would do all the better. They came with a generous breakfast of toast, eggs, bananas, papayas and a native cereal called "goi" - life was beginning to come in focus again.

The next thing we needed was sleep. This didn't come easy to the distraught missionaries, but we did manage several hours. Then we all gathered with Yoane and the church elders. What were we going to do?

To go back to Aru would be useless, and perhaps even suicidal. We would try the radio transmitters to see what was happening at Rethy. We were concerned about the children at the Academy.

Rethy was on the air at the usual time. They, too, were having problems with unscrupulous soldiers - not allowing anyone to leave the station. But news at Bunia was better. The missionaries there had been able to get "laissez passers" for all the missionaries in the whole territory.

Bunia's instruction was that all missionaries and families were to try to get to Rethy. Then the U.N. soldiers were coming the next day to lead us out in convoy.

Our problem was to get to Rethy. We would have to go through Aru, and we would certainly run into trouble there.

"But you can take the path through the jamba (jungle), and bypass Aru," suggested one of the elders. We knew the path he was talking about but it was very rough, and extremely overgrown with jungle. It was a long shot, but we were desperate. There was one dangerous spot and that was about 100 miles from Adi, a place called Djalasiga. There were many soldiers there, and they were usually very drunk and disagreeable. "God would see us through," we assured ourselves.

The trip through the jungle was slow and very tiring, but we had a good supply of water and sandwiches. After about 5 hours of almost hopeless jungle we reached the main road, only about twenty miles from Djalasiga. We stopped for lunch and a rest, and to plan our strategy for going through the danger area. God would help us. We had another prayer meeting before we started again.

We were to keep as close together as possible, despite the dust. We would travel at a high speed, and take the soldiers by surprise. Too, it was getting cooler, and it was late in the afternoon. The soldiers would likely be eating, and no doubt, good and soused. This was long before the Dukes of Hazard were conceived, but their tactics were to be our tactics. Our endocrine glands were pulsating as we neared Djalasiga in a cloud of dust.

We approached cautiously, and with as little noise as possible. Within about a half-mile from the roadblock the lead car stepped on the throttle and the two following cars kept right on his tail. The soldiers were caught completely unawares, and we sped past them and through the barrier before they had a chance to reach for their rifles. We were far down the road and the soldiers stood aghast, with mouths wide open, looking like a bunch of dummies. They would surely follow us, but by the time they got their lumbering vehicles started, we were well on our way to safer territory. About 10 miles beyond the roadblock, we relaxed our speed. Finally we stopped and the 3 cars disgorged 3 households of missionaries who just rolled over in hilarious laughter. We embraced each other and congratulated each other that we had pulled a fast one on the swashbucklers.

"But just a jolly minute!" someone reminded us, "this feat of ours could never have been pulled off successfully, without God being at the controls of each of those cars." We bowed humbly before our God, and gave Him all the praise.

We arrived at Rethy in time for a late supper, tired but elated. What a joy to be with Steve again. He, along with other academy children were enjoying this. It was a hair-raising thriller, not from a soft-cover novel, but in very real life. Most of us, oldsters, couldn't be quite that casual. We were still in Zaire, and still under the capricious care of the swashbucklers.

Early the next morning the first truck load of "blue-hat" U.N. soldiers arrived. We started to feel a little more secure. It was great to trust the Lord, but our feeble faith could also stand a little bolstering from the United Nations.

By noon there were a half dozen powerful new trucks, filled with about a hundred well-armed soldiers of different nationalities and races. There were 48 carloads of missionaries with their children loaded and ready for the 30 mile trip to the border.     Two of the U.N. trucks took their places at the head of the convoy; two more were in the ranks of the convoy; and the last two took up the rear. The motley array of soldiers and missionaries, well-armed and fortified, seemed like a sure thing. Crowds of people lined the roads - some shouting epithets of hateful abuse, and others weeping over the loss of the missionaries and the gross treatment they were receiving. As we made our way to the border there were rocks hurled into the convoy of paradoxical white people, extremely hated by some, and extravagantly loved by others.

At the Mahagi border there was a large camp of Congolese soldiers who hated the U.N. soldiers with a passion. Their feeling toward the missionaries was passionate love on one hand, and passionate hate on the other. Their inner conscience reminded them of the good they had received through the missionaries; their desire to be popular urged them to hate and abuse them.

The Congolese soldiers did not want all these white people to leave. They would come in handy as hostages. The roads were blocked, and the soldiers were hostile. They were ready to stage a massacre. The U.N. soldiers wanted at all costs to avoid bloodshed, but they were resolute. They were determined to see these missionaries through.

The blue-hatted Colonel confronted the Congolese Capitaine. "We want you to open the roadblock, and the immigration barrier so that these missionaries can pass through to Uganda. "We will do nothing of the sort," countered the Capitaine. "We have orders that no white people are to leave the country."

The impasse looked serious. The whole battery of swashbucklers were lined up for battle, anxiously waiting for the order to open fire. The Colonel tried sweet-talk and then swear-talk. He was articulate in both. The Capitaine would not budge.

The Congolese officers' patience was soon exhausted. He ordered his soldiers to remove all the missionaries from their cars, and to place them under arrest in the military camp. The U.N. Colonel ordered his soldiers to stand by to protect the missionaries, but not to attack.

The Colonel had radio transmission equipment and he reported the situation to the U.N., Headquarters at Bunia. A confrontation with the Congolese Colonel at Bunia followed. A long and loud harangue took place between these two officials. Finally they agreed to go to the scene of the incident together to investigate it. This was radioed to Mahagi - over 100 miles away.

We sat in the army camp - experiencing much the same that we had had at Aru just two days before. We were hungry and thirsty and hot. There were small children along, who were restless. Why would God allow this to happen? Should we not pray some of the imprecatory prayers of the Psalms, and ask God to strike down these wicked soldiers?

But the academy students came up with a better idea. They armed themselves with a good supply of tracts, and the Bangals magazine "Litaloi", written in Bangala, the army language, and started to circulate amongst the soldiers. This was frightening to us to see these kids begin to fraternize with the "enemy"; but the soldiers liked the tracts, and especially the magazine. It was amazing to see how our wonderful kids turned hostility into handshaking happiness.

"Hey you, Mwana (child), let me see what you've got. Can I have one?" With a complete change of attitude the soldiers dropped their rifles and reached out hungrily for the Gospel literature. Some of them were real Christians, and many more had Mission backgrounds. From then on the whole atmosphere of the camp was relaxed, and we were allowed to circulate more freely.

But as the kids collaborated, we became more hungry and thirsty. About 8 P.M. the official car from Bunia arrived with the U.N. and Congolese dignitaries. Another confrontation followed with more "sweet-talk" mixed with cursing and threatening.

About 10 P.M. the Congolese Colonel capitulated. "O.K., you may allow the cars to pass. But every car and every person must be searched thoroughly, and everyone must fill out the customs and Immigration Papers. We don't want any of these white people to run away with any of Congo's riches."

It was not until 3 A.M. until the car I was driving crossed the border into Uganda. A tremendous relief it was to see the soldier lift the barrier for us to pass. It crashed down hard again after we were through, and there were still a few of our cars behind the barrier. They all passed through soon after us. We were still in Congolese territory, but the big hurdles were behind us. Three more miles in "No Man's Land" and then another barrier.

This time it was Uganda, and the British were in control. They had been apprised of our ordeal, and they were expecting us. They had gallons of hot tea for us, and buckets of soup, with an endless supply of sandwiches. This was too much, and some of our folks broke down and wept. The British officials received us with compassion.

The cocks were crowing again. It was a new day, and we were in a free country. We were so tired that it hurt, but we were no longer afraid. But we did wonder how Yoane and all our Kakwa friends were back at Adi?

Some of our missionaries to the north did not get out in this evacuation. The Zande Land missionaries were far from the points of exit. They had started out, but there were many road blocks. They had many hassles with soldiers and they were thoroughly discouraged. In disgust they turned around and went back to their stations.

Those of us who did get out were scattered through AIM's work in Uganda, Tanzania and Kenya. After some months, things quieted down and our missionaries began to filter back into Congo again. ❖

1973 - General Lundulla presenting "Ordre du Leoparde"
from President Mubutu to Pete

## Lions On The Loose
## Chapter 16

Yoane rode the political storm after the missionaries had evacuated. There were many anxious times, but not serious enough to shake the venerable pastor's faith. From his youth he had suffered for his convictions, having been imprisoned and threatened with deportation on many occasions. "Independence" was just another chapter in the annals of his colorful career. A verse of Scripture that bolstered the underpinnings of his patriarchal peace and patience was Romans 8:37 - "In all these things we are more than conquerors."

The missionaries began to drift back from Uganda and Kenya. After several months the Peter Stams and the Bob Robinsons were again installed at Adi. They found their homes and all their belongings in good order. The Kakwa Christians had taken excellent care of things. Yoane had slept in their houses on a rotating basis each night.

It was seven months before Edythe and I could return to Zaire. We had been drafted into a teaching position at the Machokos Swahili Bible Institute in Kenya. We had to complete the school term with them.

Dr. Carl Becker was our Field Director during those days of Independence turmoil. This was far too much for the 67 year old doctor with his heavy medical schedule. In 1962 I was appointed to succeed him as Field Director. The Mission's headquarters had for several years been located at Rethy, our largest station in Zaire, situated above Lake Albert in the highlands. We were assigned to move the Field Director's office back to Rethy from Oicha where the doctor had his medical work.

Bunia was the seat of the Government's provincial headquarters. It was an attractive city of about 60,000 people, and the Belgians had paved the main street that was a mile long. They had planted rows of beautiful jacaranda and eucalyptus trees to spread their fragrance and shade through the heat of the day. A flourishing commercial center was established with supermarkets, department stores, modern garages, and hardware stores. There was an efficient Post Office with international telegraph services, and a modern airport. The homes were colonial style, made of brick, with elaborate space and exquisite furnishings. Bunia had been Belgium at its best.

The beautiful colony, with Belgians living in an exotic and luxurious life style, caused the blacks to become discontented with their lot. They saw that they were living at the extreme opposite end of the lifestyle spectrum. Discontent led to rebellion that resulted in Independence.

Independence, however, brought disillusionment. African officials, poorly equipped for their jobs, sat behind the Belgians' desks, and they became disgustingly drunk with the heady wine of power. Not only did they want their pocket to jingle with many inflated francs, but they wanted to control the lives of their fellow citizens. The politicians were a young breed, and they were having their day in court. The older Congolese tried to reason with them.

"The Belgians made our yoke grievous. Now you have the whip in your hands. They lashed us with their hippo-hide 'fimbo' and placed a heavy load on our shoulders. Now you, our sons, must make the yoke lighter. You must hang the whip on the wall and leave it there as a reminder of those bitter days. Make our life easier and we will serve you well. We will help you to build a strong independent African nation."

But like an ancient king of Israel, these politicians forsook the counsel of their elders. "The Belgians burdened you with a heavy yoke, we will make it five times as heavy. They chastised you with hippo-hide whips, we will chastise you with the fiery sting of the scorpion."

Indeed, the young officials were in the driver's seat. They began to drive recklessly and with an astonishing lack of skill. There were many serious crashes and clashes, and far too many fatalities. Many good things, such as medical help and education, were taken for granted from the Belgians. Now they were being taken away. The population had to depend on Mission hospitals and dispensaries for 90% of their medical care. About the only education available to them was to be found in the mission schools.

The swashbuckler soldiers, now impressively called the "Armee Nationale du Congo (A.N.C.)", were likewise disillusioned with the politicians. Their salaries were paid very sporadically. The strong discipline they had once seen in the Belgian Army gave way to a total lack of it. Each soldier was a law unto himself. He could commandeer a poor farmer's bicycle at will. Or he could take away a woman's basket of food that she was taking to the market in order to make a few francs to buy food for her children.

The people became very dissatisfied. Some of the older folks secretly told us that they would gladly have the Belgians back. There was extreme poverty, and this led to more crime. The prisons were so filled and so filthy that there was no room to squeeze in more. No food was served to the hapless and hopeless inmates. Unless the poor prisoners had relatives to bring them food they went hungry.

Periodically the officials called for a "Clean House Operation", in which the vast majority of prisoners were spanked, as the Belgians never would have dared to spank them, and then sent home. Home to an empty larder and with no money. This put them back on the streets to commit more crimes. They had to eat, they reasoned. How else could they survive?

These chaotic conditions prepared a very fertile field for subversive forces to penetrate. Chinese and Soviet propaganda flooded the town, blaming the Congolese's woes on American imperialism and capitalism. Chinese agents entered the country to indoctrinate and recruit a young army of rebels.

This led to a young rebel army which called itself the "Simbas" (lions). They were rabidly anti-American, and insanely obsessed with the goal of over throwing the newly independent Congolese government. They were determined to obliterate the ANC and they were going to barbecue all Americans in the country. Missionaries were the worst of the lot because they were all Agents of the American CIA, so they believed.

The Chinese Marxists also capitalized on the evils of witchcraft. The Simba Army was comprised of primitive tribesmen, led by witch doctors. Each recruit was inducted with an elaborate witchcraft ceremony. They were given a poisonous "dawa" (medicine) to rub into lacerations on their bodies, which made them immune to bullets. If they drank a small portion of this potion, it would cause the bullets to turn into water. The Simbas firmly believed this, and when one of them was shot and killed, they were told that it was because the victim had violated a taboo.

The Simbas were very successful against the ANC because the latter were nothing but a demoralized and mutinous army that would turn tail and run for a hiding place at the first sign of shooting. Or worse yet, they would turncoat and join the Simbas.

The Simbas had a war cry as they charged into battle: "Mai-Mai" (water, water), they cackled as they conquered. They smoked marijuana to give them even more courage, or hashish to make them insanely angry. To make them immune to the enemies bullets, they carried a sprig of palm branch in their cap or shirt, if they were fortunate enough to have a cap or shirt. If not, they stuck it into their kinky hair. When they shot or captured a white man they would not touch his body, thinking that such physical contact would nullify their magic immunity to bullets. The Simbas were very successful throughout the east section of Zaire. In July, 1964 they captured the provincial Capital of Kindu. From there they pushed on to Stanleyville, now known as Kisangani. The battle of that city has been graphically told by David Reed in his book "111 Days in Stanleyville". Dr. Paul Carlson was catapulted into the world spotlight during that time, being shot by the Simbas. Many missionaries, about 40 in all, were also killed by Simbas in that battle.

From Stanleyville they pushed north to Isiro, and up to the Central African Republic on the north; and east to the Sudan and Uganda borders. The Simbas were atrocious and grossly cruel, killing, mutilating, beating and raping both white people, and their own blacks. The story of this rebellion is a significant chapter in the annals of modern martyrdom and cruelty.

However, all this was far removed from Adi. The Simba rebellion would be quashed long before it would reach the area of the Kakwas, some 700 miles away from Stanleyville. Missionaries would hang in there and ride out this wave of trouble. There had been two evacuations during the events following Independence. None of the African church leaders or missionaries had been hurt. God would see us through this ordeal too. "I shall not be moved," became one of our favorite hymns.

We should have our suitcases packed and be ready to move in a moments notice if necessary. In the meantime, we would keep on working and planning as though we had another 50 years. We read
Psalm 121 - "my help cometh from the Lord — He shall not suffer thy foot to be moved".

Little did we realize that the Simbas would reach our area so soon. Al Larson, Field Director of the Unevangelized Fields Mission in the Stanleyville area, still had his radio transmitter, and was still able to communicate over the 700 miles of forest to us at Rethy. "K M 8. calling Rethy" he came in loud and clear, "inform all U.F.M. missionaries to evacuate into Uganda immediately. Do you read me? Over."

"Roger, Roger, K M 8 - Rethy reads you. Will pass your message along. But is the situation that serious that they should leave? Over."

"Roger, Rethy. This problem is different from anything we have seen before. My advice is that all you AIM missionaries should also leave as quickly as possible. You do not - I repeat - you do not have much time. The American Consul here, Michael Hoyt, confirms this message. Do you read me, Rethy? Over."

"Roger K M 8, we read you. What about all you missionaries in the Stanleyville area? Can you also come out this way? Over."

"Negative, we cannot leave. We are under house-arrest. This, no doubt, will be our last opportunity to communicate with you. Get out fast, or you will be in the same situation. Must terminate communication. This is K M 8 over, and out."

"Roger, K M 8. We shall be praying for you. Read Psalm 46, and keep trusting. He is sovereign. This is Rethy, over and out." This radio contact came in as a breaker into our AIM net during the daily one o'clock schedule. All our missionaries heard the message, and reactions were mixed. Some thought we were pushing the panic button, and that it was not necessary to evacuate. The majority, however, thought we should go as soon as possible.

Over our radio net we decided that we should pray over it through the night, and then come on the air again at 8:30 the next morning. Needless to say, there were very few who slept well that night. None of us really wanted to go to Kenya or Uganda again, and leave the African Church to go through this alone. Nor did we relish the idea of a barbecue with missionaries on the spit. We prayed.

Dawn finally broke with the cocks entirely unaware, or concerned, about the Simba situation. Their cacophony was as raucous as ever. Just another day for the roosters. At 8 o'clock the American Consul broke into our usual morning net. "Breaker, Breaker! - This is the American Consul at Kampala. I have a message for Brashler."

His message came through loud and clear. "Roger, Mr. Consul, we read you loud and clear. Go ahead with your message. Over"

"We have information about the lions (Simbas) that you perhaps do not have. The Simbas are on their way into your area, coming from the North through Watsa and Aba, and from the South through Bunia. You have a very short time to get out of the country." He emphatically told us that this was urgent, and if we wanted to avoid the spit over the barbecue, we had better take his words seriously.

Obviously, the Consul's message helped us to make up our minds. We decided that we would not leave in convoy, as that would attract too much attention, and somebody, perhaps all, would get hurt. My final instruction was, "Pack as lightly and as quickly as possible, leave one car at a time at varied intervals. Don't panic. Keep trusting, and may God bless you and keep you."

Before signing off, I read Jeremiah 39:17-18. "I will deliver you in that day, and thou shalt not be given into the hand of the men of whom thou art afraid. For I will surely deliver you, and thou shalt not fall by the sword - because thou hast put thy trust in me."

All of these events have been recorded more fully in my book "CHANGE" in Chapter 18, titled "Get Out While You Still Can". All our AIM missionaries evacuated safely with the exception of the Chuck Davis family who had been assigned to the Stanleyville area to teach in the Inter-Mission Theological Seminary. Chuck and his wife, Muriel, who was 6 months pregnant with their third child, along with their first two children were caught behind the Simba lines for three months, most of which time was spent under house arrest.

Toward the end of that period Chuck was imprisoned in Stanleyville, along with all the other male American missionaries. The final day of their Simba Saga came on Nov. 24, 1964, when wave after wave of mercenary paratroopers, hired by the Central Government in Kinshasa, dropped on the Stanleyville Airport early in the morning.

As soon as the Simbas realized what was taking place they herded all the hostages out of the prison and the various hotels in which they were kept. They marched the prisoners to the town square where they were all to be executed before the paratroopers could fight their way into town.

Chuck Davis and Paul Carlson had had their devotions together in prison before the Paratrooper Pandemonium broke loose. Chuck had read to Carlson from Proverbs 24 - "Rejoice not when thine enemy falleth, and let not thine heart be glad when he stumbleth".

"You know, Paul," Chuck said to the doctor, "I have a premonition that today this whole nightmare will be over. I believe God is going to deliver us."

"I wish I could share that feeling with you Chuck. I have the strong impression that today I'm going to meet my Lord. My only concern now is for my wife and children. I pray that God will make His Grace sufficient for them in their every need." The doctor was at peace about his own fate, but deeply concerned over his loved ones.

They were being rushed by the Simbas to the place of their death. Chuck and Paul trudged along side by side. Both of them clutched their Bibles to their sides. Chuck had taken his toothbrush along. He was still expecting a miraculous deliverance.

There were well over 200 hostages being marched as sheep to the slaughter. Many of them were women with screaming babes in their arms. The Colonel in charge, Colonel Opepe, had his automatic rifle slung over his shoulder, as he marched beside the doomed prisoners. He personally had shown at least a semblance of kindness. He was really sorry to see it end this way.

The city still had its natural beauty. Poinsettia bushes stood tall and stately in warm contrasted colors. The frangipangi trees lining the thoroughfares smiled fragrantly and benevolently on the hapless hoard of doomed men, women and children, some of them marching stoically to their rendezvous with their Maker; others cursing, others praying, some weeping silently, others screaming. Exotic birds, dressed in feathers of every imaginable hue, were flying in every direction, sounding out the death knell, as though they were protesting to the Simbas. The procession continued silently in its funeral march as the Simbas jeered and taunted the tormented and terrorized throng.

The procession was suddenly shocked into an electrified halt. The Simbas and the hostages stood rigid under the loud blast of gunfire. The paratroopers were only a few hundred yards away. Colonel Opepe ordered the prisoners to sit down on the streets, hoping secretly that many of them would thus be saved from the flying bullets. Many of the Simbas ran for cover, deserting their cause.

One Simba teenager pointed his rifle into the crowd and fired at random. Many others fired into the mass of hostages, killing a large number. It sounded like the cohorts of hell had broken loose, bent on destroying all the hostages. Chuck and Carlson scrambled to their feet and ran for the shelter of an abandoned Belgian bungalow with a veranda and a brick banister around it. Chuck being agile, scaled the wall and dropped behind the banister. For the moment he was safe from the Simba machine gun fire.

Paul Carlson was right at Chuck's heels, and Chuck reached out for Paul's hands to pull him up over the banister. Just as he was being helped over the wall a barrage of bullets bit into his back. He died instantly. Chuck, crushed and devastated, had to let the dead doctor fall to the ground outside the banister.

The Paratroopers routed the Simbas in a very short time. The Davis family were reunited in Kinshasa. Al Larson and the surviving U.F.M. missionaries were likewise rescued. Other U.F.M'ers were delivered in the weeks to follow. Over twenty of the U.F.M. missionaries were killed by the Simbas.

This had been an extremely bad time for the missionaries, especially those who suffered at the hands of the Simbas. But it was extremely worse for the African Pastors and Church leaders. Most of them had no way to escape the cruel caprice of these Satan-inspired rebels. Many hundreds of them were killed, and others imprisoned and beaten. The country was lacerated under the spear and sword of the Simbas.

We followed all these events on the safe sides of the Uganda and Kenya borders. We wept over the fate of many of our dear missionary friends who lost their lives. Some whole families were executed. We wept even more because of the church leaders who were still being crushed under the guerrilla warfare that the Simbas were waging out in the jungle country. How could this beloved church, to whom we had, by then, given a quarter of a century of our lives, survive?

We underestimated the church. When the missionaries left the leaders rallied the believers together in Pentecost prayer meetings. Yoane led the leaders at Adi in planning for the future. "I must work the works of Him that sent me while it is day" was his theme verse.

"But the Simbas will kill us if they see us carry on the work of the missionaries," objected a few. "We must keep a low profile for a while."

"Oyo nini? (What's this I hear)," exclaimed Yoane. This is

not the work of the missionaries. This is God's work, and we are His workmen. We shall have our public services as we have been accustomed to having them. We shall preach to the Simbas. They need it more than our own people do. "The Lord is on our side; we will not fear what the Simbas can do to us" paraphrased the pastor.

That was the pattern they followed. Life as usual. Large services were held each week, danger and dying, and devilish Simbas lurking on in the background notwithstanding. Many leaders were arrested and beaten and held in prison, but the Christians prayed. They told us about it later when we returned, "Oh Bwana and Madame, during those days we held all-night prayer meetings in many of the huts. Only we didn't pray anymore. Those prayers we used to say were so empty in the face of what was happening; they sounded like the rattle of the dancer's drum. When we saw what was happening to our brothers and sisters we just didn't pray; we began to talk to God."

There was indeed a falling away of a few of the faint-hearted. The true believers, however, "walked not after the counsel of the ungodly; they stood not in the way of sinners; nor sat in the seat of the scornful. Their delight was in the Law of the Lord." Psalm 1:1-2

"But the ungodly were not so - they were like the chaff that the wind drives away." Psalm 1:4

The wheat was sifted and the chaff was blown away. The true church stood strong, and actually grew under persecution. ❖

Duck bill of the Babira Tribe in Bunia, Zaire

# Bearding the Lion and Twisting His Tail
## Chapter 17

The Simbas, like the lions of the jungle, whose Swahili name they bare, were on a roaring rampage. The missionaries had all evacuated from Adi leaving their homes and all their belongings in the hands of Yoane and the church leaders.

"Don't worry," said Yoane as they were leaving, "We'll guard your houses with our lives."

Later the Simbas came to Adi to see if there were still any missionaries. They searched the houses, Yoane leading them with a Simba behind him with a gun in his back. The Simbas were mad because the whites had all gotten away. Yoane and the elders were made scapegoats.

They started the search in Peter and Mary Lou Stam's house. They went through every nick and corner, breaking windows and doors and furniture as they went from room to room. They found a box of rifle ammunition that Peter had over looked— "Aha! You have ammunition hidden here. Where are the guns?"

"No guns, and no more ammunition, "replied Yoane calmly. The chief knows that all guns and ammunition were confiscated during the time of Independence."

"Yoane," the captain roared, "you are trying my patience. You tell us where the guns are hidden, or I will dissect your body right here, and leave the pieces for the hyenas to find tonight."

"Fine," retorted Yoane, "I would like to go to heaven. I have had my fill of this world. Especially since you, Simbas, have taken over and made such a mess of it."

"Mind your tongue, you black Macaque, (monkey) or I will cut it out and make you swallow it. Where are those guns?"

"There are none! - Search all that you like, but you won't find any."

The Simba was seething in anger. His eyes fell on Yoane's ears with the large keloid growths. To one of the other Simbas he said, "cut off his miserable ears.- They look like a pair of kidneys turned inside out. Where he's going he won't need any ears.

"Then if he doesn't tell us where the guns are" continued the Simba, "We will cut off his nose, then his eyes. Piece by piece we will leave his miserable carcass to the buzzards. Unless, of course, he tells us where the guns are. Then we will give him a dignified death by cutting his head off."

"Kill me any way you want to," replied Yoane, "but what I tell you is true. There are no guns. Kill me and I will go straight to heaven. I'm not afraid to die. What about you? You, too, will die and perhaps sooner than you think. Then you will stand before my Father in heaven. He will judge you for your wickedness. He will have a place all prepared for you. It will be a large lake of fire into which He will throw you to burn forever. — Is that what you want?"

"If not," continued Yoane with holy boldness, "Then you better repent right now, and believe in Jesus Who is my Savior. He wants to be your Savior too. After you have killed me, you better find the Elders of the church. They will tell you how to be saved from that lake of fire, and will receive you as brothers."

"Now, Mr. Simba, if you are going to kill me, I am ready. Do it any way you want to. I will pray for you while I am dying, and I will show you how a Christian can die."

Actually the Simba had been reluctant all the time to kill Yoane. One who audaciously dared to defy the Simba, and literally laughed at the horrendous death they were capable of inflicting on their victims, must be a demigod. These Kakwa Christians unflinchingly stared death in the face and shook a stick at it. The Simbas believed that Yoane had the heart of a lion beating in his breast. They themselves might bear the name "Simba", the terror of the jungle, but the true spirit of the conquering lion was with the Christians. No wonder Yoane was not afraid to beard the lion and twist the tail of these pitiful parodies who pretended to be Simbas.

"We must go back to Kumuru," said the Simba, "Our Colonel has arrived. We shall be back tomorrow and we shall not rest peaceably until we see the sands on which Yoane has walked all his life lap up the blood that now flows through Yoane's veins."

With a maddening roar and screams of frustration, the Simbas drove back to the Chief's village. The Christians gathered in the Chapel to praise God that Yoane was still alive, and to pray for full deliverance. "Yoane, our dear Pastor," counselled the Elders, "if they find you here tomorrow they will surely kill you. You must leave at midnight and hide out in the huts of the Christians. You can hide in the day time, and make your way to Uganda by night."

"What mean you to break my heart?" Answered Yoane in the words of Paul, the Apostle, "I am ready not only to be tortured, but also to die for the Name of Christ. If I run away they will take vengeance on you."

After many tears the Adi Christians replied with the answer of the Christians at Caesarea, "The will of the Lord be done". (Acts 21:13-14)

After more prayer they realized how hungry they were. Yoane's wife, like Martha of Bethany, invited all the Elders into her home and served them. Along with millet fufu she had a steaming pot of sweet potatoes, delicious roasted bananas and a large pot of chicken, — no doubt a couple of those who had crowed so raucously in the morning to disturb their sleep. The preachers were get-ting even with those noisy birds. They ate vociferously. They sipped their tea, they burped noisily to let Maria know how much they appreciated the meal. They even laughed as they rehearsed the awkwardness of the Simbas — the way they boggled their eyes when Yoane was telling them about the lake of fire. One last prayer and they all slept - snoringly, snortingly, and above all "soundly". It sounded like a sawmill, and they were making the best use of the time Yoane had left. The Simbas were back at 7 A.M. "Where's Yoane?" they demanded of the few who had the courage to come out and meet them.

"Yoane is still sleeping."

"What?" Roared the amazed lion. He just could not understand that man. How could he sleep in the face of the fate awaiting him? This aggravated the Simba, making him realize that he was dealing with a different breed of cat than the cowardly Simbas.

Yoane finally appeared with the Elders. He invited the Simba leaders to the veranda of the old Station house. "Some tea?" Yoane asked quietly. "Sure," he replied. He might be a Simba, but at least he was still the old gregarious African of better days. He was jovial as he drank the tea.

"Where's the bankie?" demanded the Simba, suddenly changing his attitude, and forgetting entirely the gun fiasco of the day before.

"There is no bankie (money)," responded Yoane, "all the missionaries' money was used up to pay teachers' and nurses'salaries. We are broke."

"Monsieur," bristled the Simba, "The American Capitalists had plenty of money. Where is it?"

Repeat performance of yesterday, thought Yoane. "I'm sorry Monsieur, there is no bankie. The money is all gone."

From the joviality of the teapot to the jungle terror of the Simba world, the Simba began to curse. — "Yoane, you have tried my patience to the limit. You bring the bankie out or I will kill you now. You make me sick the way you calmly shake a stick at death, and the way you can sleep all night while I lie awake tossing. I've had it with you, Preacher." — Grabbing his rifle, he pointed it at Yoane.

"Oh wait, Bwana! cried Catherine, "I can bring you the bankie."

Catherine, a mulatto lady, was a nurse on the station. She sprang between the Simba and her very dear friend, Yoane. She wanted at all costs to save his life.

Catherine was born of a Congolese mother, and an aristocratic Greek father who had been a wealthy merchant in Congo before Independence. This Greek had come from Greece to Africa to make his fortune like most Greeks, he was a very astute business man. He made a large fortune, and money was the one thing in life he respected.

To alleviate his loneliness he bought an African wife. She was beautiful and fabulously formed. Her body reminded him of a Greek goddess. He paid his bride's father a generous dowry, and he was happy with his black bride. Catherine and her young sister, Fitinia were two beautiful half cast children that issued from this union.

The Greek brought his girls to the mission station when they were 6 and 8 years old respectively. They were smart, and learned quickly. Catherine became a nurse and worked at the Adi Dispensary. Fitinia, like her father, had an eye for a fast buck. She had a lucrative bakery in Bunia.

Now Catherine bearded the lion and was ready to twist his tail. She wanted to save Yoane's life.

"What Pastor says is true, Bwana. He does not have the money. If you want the bankie, I can give it to you. — It's in my house." She lied with a straight face.

What she had in her house was an accumulation of her own money. She had frugally set it aside for a rainy day. She never dreamed that she might use it as a ransom to save her Pastor's life.

"You wait a few minutes and I will have the bankie here."

The Simba was placated for the moment and agreed to amoratorium of ten minutes on Yoane's execution. In five minutes she was back with a bulging flour sack. She handed it to the Simba; "Voila, Monsieur, there's your bankie."

Ungraciously he grabbed the sack and poured its contents on the floor. He counted about 3000 francs, which was a large sum for those days.

"Where's the rest?" he sneered. "The rich Americans certainly left more than this."

"That is all," she convincingly lied. "Now if you want to kill somebody you must kill me. I am the one who held the bankie."

The Simba was stumped. Catherine was half white and beautiful, and a friend of the Americans. Everything that Simbas hated. —Why didn't he shoot her? He wanted to but something was holding him back. She had the same affect on him that Yoane had. He was afraid of her.

"Yoane is going to Kumuru with me," roared the Simba. The "Colonel" is there, and he will decide how Yoane is to die. Get into the Jeep, Yoane. I want to see the color of your blood."

Yoane was not to be hurried. "Obangi te (Do not fear)," he told the Adi Saints. "I am not afraid to die. Keep on doing

God's work. Don't grieve over me, my brothers and sisters. God will let you live on earth yet for a while because He has a work for you to do. Don't let anyone drive you out of God's will for you. When your work is completed we shall all be together with the Savior. Don't follow me to Kumuru. You must not see me die. I won't need a funeral. The Simbas will throw my body into the Nzoro River and the crocodiles will eat it. It's best that way. Good bye, my beloved, and God bless and keep you."

The jeep roared off to Kumuru with Yoane squeezed between two Simbas — filthy and foul and rancid. Yoane's shirt was clean, and his neat khaki shorts clean and properly pressed. As he sped over the familiar five miles he had no time for nostalgia or self-pity. He was going to meet the self-styled "Colonel", who would question him. What kind of man would he be? How would he best be able to witness to him about Christ?

The Christians remained at Adi as Yoane had instructed. They were gripped with grief over their beloved Pastor's fate. "Was God sure He knew what was happening? - Was this really the end for Yoane? Had God forsaken them?

Then they remembered Yoane's words: "I will be fine! Keep on doing God's work. Don't let anyone drive you out of God's will. We shall all be together again."

God had not forsaken them. All this was God's doing and He had an inconceivable purpose in it all. God was allowing this.

But Yoane was still alive! Perhaps even yet God would deliver him. They all gathered together in the Chapel to begin their prayer vigil.

Yoane arrived at the Chief's compound, as casual as though he were going to a market meeting. A large crowd had gathered, somewere his enemies who wanted to see the sands red with Yoane's blood. Most of them were very dear friends who came to pray, and to stand with him through this ordeal.

The Colonel, who was regarded as the Simba's superstar, gathered the chiefs together with the Simba leaders. They were dressed in full regalia of Simba insignia — strips of leopard skins, lion claws dangling around their necks, monkey feet tied in their belts, lavish headdresses of every shape and color, decorated with exotic bird feathers. All the insignia had some evil spirit significance.

A large platform of poles and elephant grass had been erected, around which the crowd gathered. It was about ten feet high. The Simba Colonel mounted the superstructure to address the vast crowd. He was an orator extraordinaire. Yoane's hands were tied as he stood at the foot of the platform.

The Simba on his perch began his harangue: "All white people are very bad. Only the devil could conceive a man with white skin and straight blond hair. The worst ones among them are the missionaries. They must all die. Even our own black Pastors who have been in league with the missionaries must die, and also the church Elders."

"If the Kakwa people," he continued, "will destroy the Church that Americans started, and will cooperate with the Simbas in getting rid of all undesirables, then they will have a good country. There will be no rich people, and no poor people - all will share alike. The wealth of the filthy rich will be evenly divided among all Simba supporters. Our enemies will die without mercy. All doctors and nurses will be kept alive to be slaves of the Simbas. The Armies of the Simbas will rule the earth. Life will be good."

The harangue was interminable. Many Kakwas were yawning. They had heard enough. Many wanted to hear Yoane scream, and see his blood flow, like a scarlet spring of water. They had come to see the execution. But on and on went the monologue.

"We will cleanse our country from the filth of the Capitalists. We will kill all the old chiefs along with all pastors and elders. We will purify our country."

The Simbas standing below the Colonel's perch interrupted the orator. "Yeah! Yeah! — We will kill. But now we want to see Yoane's blood. Let us start with this preacher. — Kill him! Kill him! —"

The Colonel on his perch got the message. These mawkish Monsters, below him, had heard enough blah. — Now they wanted blood. "Very well" responded the Colonel, "We shall hear his screams and see his blood."

He was not too enthusiastic about this because he had heard much about Yoane, who shook a stick at death. He was not one bit intimidated by the sadomasochism of the murderous Simbas. This frustrated the Colonel, and he'd like to sidestep this issue of executing Yoane, even though he hated Yoane with a passion. In spite of his Marxist indoctrination, he was still African enough to believe in God.

"We want Yoane!" screamed the crowd of Simbas. They were getting impatient. Yoane felt that his time was up, so signaled with his tied hands to the Simba on the perch, indicating that he wanted to speak his last message.

"Yoane, you shall have your last chance to speak, but I want everyone to hear you and see you. You have been an important Pastor so I want you to come up on this platform and say what you have to say."

No way could he climb that high mount with his hands tied. The super Simba gave instructions that the ropes on his wrists should be cut. The Simba leader climbed down and Yoane climbed up. Facing the masses below, he saw that the majority were his friends and supporters. The noisy minority, however, took charge, and they wanted his blood, they finally settled down to hear Yoane speak.

"Mbote Mingi, baninga na ngai (greetings to you my many friends)," he said with a smile. "I want to thank the Colonel forgiving me permission to speak. Many of you have heard me preach about Yesu Kristu. You know that I am not afraid to die. Today you will kill my body, but I myself will go to heaven. You who are really Christians will see me again. I beg you Christians not to be afraid. Follow Jesus until you, too, join me in heaven.

"What I really want to say in my last message is for you who are Simbas. Many of you are Kakwas, and I have known you for forty years. You have been my neighbors and friends. You call yourselves Simbas or lions. You behave like lions because you bring terror into the villages. You are strong because you are many and you are united in your evil deeds. You strike terror because you torture and kill innocent people."

"Let me tell you a story about one of God's Pastors, named Daniel. He told the people that unless they followed God they would be banished from God forever. This made many people very angry, and the accused him falsely to the king, who agreed that such a person should die in the lions' pit. When the king realized that the man he had condemned was Daniel, he tried to deliver him. However, the sentence of death had been signed and sealed. He could not change it.

"Daniel was thrown into the lions' pit. He was not afraid of the beasts because he knew God was with them. He fell right in the middle of a pack of the greatest and most ferocious lions he had ever seen. He lay on the bottom of the pit, waiting for the lions to attack. To his amazement the beasts lay down beside him and went to sleep. The mass of people stood spell bound as Yoane warmed up to his sermon. He felt perfectly at ease because he was doing what he liked best — preach to sinners. The Simbas had never heard such a story, told with such passion and power.

"The lions slept through the night," Yoane continued his message, "It was cold in the dungeon so Daniel sidled up to the lions. The beasts were perfectly content to provide a warm, comfortable bed for Daniel. One of the old males offered him his long mane for a soft pillow.

"The King couldn't sleep that night because he knew that Pastor Daniel was a man of God. — He spent the night fasting and praying. Before the first cock of the morning crowed he found his way to the lions' den. 'Oh Daniel,' he cried, 'has your God been able to save you?' Daniel replied sleepily, getting up from his warm bed, "Oh King, don't worry about me. God has sent his angel to close the mouths of these lions. I am not in the least bit hurt."

"The King had Daniel hoisted out of the pit. He was so relieved to see Daniel unharmed... then he arrested the enemies of the Pastor and had them thrown to the beasts. The powerful creatures had these wicked men torn limb from limb before they ever fell to the bottom of the den. t h e y had a great feast."

Yoane continued his message: "I don't know if God will

deliver me from the claws of the Simbas today. But I do know that it is appointed to all people to die, and after death, to judgment. You must all die, and you too, will have to stand before God, the Judge. Unless you repent, He will throw you into the den of the Roaring Lion, the devil. God loves you Simbas, He gave His only Son to die for your sins. If you believe you will have life everlasting."

The Simbas were entranced as Yoane finished his sermon. The Colonel wanted to release him, but that would cause him to lose face. What could he do?

He decided to ignore Yoane's sermon. There would be another way to save face. "Yoane" he said, "you have been a good Pastor and helped many people. Now I want you to help me. I need guns and ammunition. If you will bring me the missionaries' guns, then I may be able to release you. Where are those guns?"

"Mais M. le Colonel, I don't know where those guns are. They were confiscated four years ago at the time of Independence. That is the truth. Chief Drupa can corroborate my statement."

"Yoane, if you don't produce those guns then I will have to shoot you," said the Colonel dolefully. — He was trying to save Yoane's life, and his own face.

The Simba soldiers had been impressed with Yoane's message, and they, too, were reluctant to kill him, who was on such good terms with God.

Yoane, still on top of his perch, answered the Colonel, "I have told you the truth. If you are going to shoot me, then start shooting. Why do you waste any more time on me?"

"Very well, Yoane," replied the Colonel, and turning to the Simba soldiers, "Shoot him!" Six Simbas aimed their rifles up to Yoane and started shooting. — With the first shot, Yoane winced, grasping his shoulder. He slumped to his knees and fell on the elephant grass carpet on the perch gasping for breath. There were six shots in all, and Yoane counted them. He must be severely hurt, he thought, because he could feel nothing. But he didn't die! The Simbas had come shockingly close to him but they all missed him. He wasn't even scratched.

Yoane got to his feet and started to taunt the soldiers. "What kind of soldiers are you? If you can't shoot better than that, then you better turn in your rifles. If you are going to send me to heaven then please take a better aim. Here I am — Shoot me!"

Yoane sensed that they had deliberately missed him. They wanted to scare him. The Colonel ordered him down from his perch. He was absolutely frustrated.— How should the Colonel of the Simba army deal with a character like Yoane!

"I am going to let you go back to Adi for today," said the Colonel, "while I consider your case. — Your people must see you die."

The Saints at Adi were still keeping their prayer vigil. They had prayed through the noon hour. About one o'clock they heard the shooting from Kumuru. They heard all six shots in succession. They were sure it was all over for Yoane. They were struck with grief and they kept on praying for another hour. While still in the Chapel they heard a crowd of shouting people coming toward Adi. These must be the mourners, coming with the details of Yoane's death. As they came closer, however, the Saints realized that the shouting crowd was not mourning, but rejoicing. This was definitely not a mourner's dirge.

As the crowd reached the Chapel they saw Yoane leading the pack. "He's alive! He's alive!" The sad meeting suddenly turned into one of rejoicing, with shouts of praise, and songs of gladness. — "Yoane was alive!"

That afternoon the Saints gathered again for a strategy meeting. Yoane's life had been spared for the moment, the roaring lions had stepped on the branch of a thorn tree. Their paws were hurting, and they were mad. Tomorrow there would be a massacre.

It was decided that Yoane and all the Elders should flee into the jungle, and work their way into Uganda.

Late that evening Yoane and the leaders, with a minimum of luggage tied in their nap sacks, left Adi. Each one chose his own devious route, as it would be safer to be alone. They all had many friends where they could find shelter and food.

There were many Rahabs who, like in Joshua's day, hid the spies during the day, and sent them off under the cover of darkness.

Within three days the stalwart leaders were all safe in Uganda. — The Simbas arrived at Adi the next day to find them gone. The Simbas roared ferociously, and they wrought havoc in the houses of the missionaries, taking what they wanted, and destroying the rest. The station was deserted, and the Kakwa Christians scattered, it seemed an apparent defeat for the church, but they took great comfort in Psalm 91:11-13

"He shall give His angels charge over thee to keep Thee — Thou shalt tread upon the lion and adder: The young lion and the dragon shalt thou trample under feet." ❖

## Russian Roulette
## Chapter 18

Adi had settled down to a ghost town. The missionary homes stood in disarray, with none but a few Simbas occupying them. These rebels struck havoc in every direction.

A fierce rainstorm lashed out against this desolation one evening, bringing with it a cool wind. The Simbas thought it was cold and decided to build a fire. They had already used up all the firewood left by the missionaries.

This dilemma was soon remedied by hacking up some of the nice furniture left behind. A beautiful table was turned over and the legs of it were chopped off. To build a fire, however, they needed kindling and paper. This need was met by tearing sections of pages out of the many valuable books that still lined the shelves. More of the dining room tables were chopped up for kindling. Soon they had a roaring fire that made the house much too warm for comfort.

During the time the Simbas occupied the Adi houses they demolished all the furniture. They broke every window, smashing every pane and burning the sash for firewood. They tore all the doors off their hinges, leaving gaping holes, and making the houses look like skeletons. Whatever equipment was left by the missionaries, was either destroyed or appropriated by the Simbas.

At Rethy, the station from which we evacuated, the situation was the same. I had left a library of several thousand choice books in my study in the office building. I had locked the doors, but this posed no problems for the Simbas. They simply shot out the locks. They had the idea that we had hidden money inside the books. They systematically tore sections of pages, leaving mounds of theology, history, philosophy, psychology, anthropology, and what have you. What desecration! This, I felt, was my greatest loss in the Simba destruction. Edythe didn't agree with me, thinking the loss of her furniture, dishes, crystal ware, silverware, and what more have you, were her greatest loss. When we returned, however, we could look on all those treasures as mere things.

Rethy station was where the Academy for missionaries' children was located. The Academy owned a large herd of choice, upgraded dairy cows. When the Simbas took over they welcomed the sight of well-fed and well-bred cows. For them it meant a source of fresh meat.

They took great sport in machine gunning a number of these bovine creatures everyday, cutting out only the hind quarters, loins, kidneys, livers, heart and other choice morsels. The rest of the carcasses were left right where they had fallen for predatory animals to come and have their feast in the darkness.

They did not have enough ammunition, however, to waste on cows. They must save this for any natives that might try to run away. It was more fun to shoot fleeing humans than cows. So they solved their meat problem by roping the creatures and bull-dogging them, as they had seen pictures of American cowboys doing. Once they got the cow down they began to cut off the hind quarters and the other choice portions. This they did while the cows were still alive. Some of our African friends were hiding out in the attics of some of the buildings. They saw what was going on and told us about it when we returned. The bawling of the miserable cattle was something terrible, even to Africans who are not at all squeamish about the inhuman treatment of animals. Gory stories of horror could fill volumes, all bearing out the Scriptural truth that "the heart is deceitful above all things and desperately wicked".

The Catholic nuns felt that they should not leave their posts in the convents. They were God's holy children, doing God's holy work. God would protect them.

The Simbas had another idea. They arrested all remaining Catholic missionaries, both priests and nuns, who stayed in Bunia. Some were taken to the Papa Nongovitch Hotel in the center of town. They were used as toys for the Simbas, to be played with publicly in the large lounge before the wicked eyes of crowds of Simbas. The Greek manager of the hotel told us when we returned that these lovely nuns who had taken vows of celibacy, were raped again and again, being passed from one sick Simba to the next. Beautiful nuns sanctified as God's missionaries, serving Him in a most holy and devout manner, were thus violated.

After the Simbas had sated their vile passions, and had done what would seem to be their most damnable worst, they left them bleeding and crying on the floor like crushed and crumpled flowers. The Simbas had had their fill of evil, sensual lust, but their appetites for evil were not satisfied. They turned their machine guns on the nuns and began to spit fiery lead into their bodies, leaving some of them dead on the floor. The Greek owner telling us the story would still burst into tears, a year and a half later, as he told us the story, and showed us the bullet holes in the building.

Yoane and all the Church leaders from Adi were able to escape into Uganda. Most of the Christians, however, were either prevented from crossing the border, or elected to stay in Zaire. Some of our African pastors went as missionaries to Watsa, and were there for the evil events of the Simbas. They saw more priests, nuns, Greek merchants and Belgian plantation owners herded into trucks. They were driven to the Nzoro River, about 10 kilometers from Watsa. They were lined up on the river bank and massacred by menacing machine gun fire. Many bodies fell into the river to be snapped up almost immediately into the jaws of the voracious crocodiles that infested the river. Others of the blasted bodies were grotesquely left on the river bank, waiting to be despicably devoured by hateful hyenas that were waiting for the darkness.

The Kakwa missionaries in Bunia fared no better. Mr. and Mrs. Paul Stough had evacuated into Uganda, leaving their house completely furnished and supplied, in the hands of faithful Christians.

There were two missionaries from the U.F.M. who had disregarded Director Al Larson's order to evacuate. They were affectionately called Ma and Pa Kerry, instead of their proper Scottish name Kerrigan. They were guests in our home at Rethy until we evacuated. "Pa Kerry," I said to him after Al Larson's directive, "we are all going to evacuate, and you and Ma Kerry will have to go with us."

The scraggly Scott spoke with a delightful Scottish burr, "Ach, Mon, are ye afrrraid to die for Chrrrist? I'm no goin."

I suppose if it were really necessary to die for "Chrrrist," I would "no be afrrraid", but if it's all the same, I would prefer to serve Him on earth yet for a while. I tried to communicate this to Pa Kerry, but he had a one-track Scot's mind. "I'm no goin!"

I had no jurisdiction to issue orders to U.F.M. missionaries, but I tried to reason with him. "Brrrother Brrrashlerr," he burred, "I can understand your concerrrn, but Ma Kerry and I both feel strongly that we should stay. We have prayed about it and our minds are made up. We're no goin. We want to get back to our people in Stanleyville. What we would like is your permission to stay in your Bunia House until a way opens up for us to get back to our people."

"Very well, Pa Kerry. I know you have prayed earnestly. If you really feel that you must stay then you are welcome to use the Bunia House for as long as you need it. We shall pray for you. God bless you."

Pa and Ma Kerry got to the Bunia House a few days later, and settled in for the duration. They lived there for several months, going to town everyday, well armed, not with pistols, but with Gospel tracts in Swahili and Bangala. The Simbas found out that the Kerrys were neither Belgian nor Americans, so they left them pretty much alone.

The Kerrigans, however, did not leave the Simbas alone. They barraged them daily with their own ammunition from God's Word. When they saw a group of Simbas, they preached to them in no "uncerrrtain terrrms". Ma Kerry particularly was a hellfire evangelist, and the Simbas did not know what to make of her. They all respected her, and many of them were afraid of her.

One night at about 2 A.M. a group of Simbas, dazed on drugs and zapped on booze, pounded on the front door of the house. Pa didn't hear because he never wore his hearing aid at night. His Scottish nature would not allow him to waste the batteries. Ma decided to ignore it, and turned over to go to sleep.

The Simbas persisted, however. Stupefied and befuddled, they were mad. "Ma Kerry" they screeched, "you open the door or we will blow your house away".

Ma, thoroughly disgusted, stormed out to the front door that was strongly bolted from within. "You, filthy Simbas, get out of here or I'll come out there and thrash each one of you like you've never been spanked before."

The Simbas were not easily frightened. "You open that door Ma Kerry, or we will burn your house down."

"What do you want, you wretched Simbas? Whatever it is I won't give it to ye. Be gone with ye miserable wretches."

"Ma Kerry, we have come to kill you. How can we kill you if you don't open the door? We are going to kill both you and your husband. Open the door! I command you in the name of the Simbas."

"I'll no open the door to the likes of ye. It's two o'clock in the morning, and this is no time to come and kill people. If you want to kill us, come back at 10 o'clock in the morning. I'll fix ye a wee cup of tay. After that ye can kill us. Now get out of here."

Ma shuffled back to her bedroom to join her snoring Scot, wondering which noise was worse - that of the sottish Simba or that of her snoring mate. She didn't want to wake him up to tell him of the incident.

The frustrated Simbas kept pounding at the door, and shouting out all manner of threats. Wearied, and at the point of passing out, they finally staggered off. By 10 o'clock when they should have been joining Ma Kerry for a "wee cup'o tay" they were all dead to the world in a stupefied sleep. By the time they awakened they had forgotten about Ma Kerry. And Ma Kerry had forgotten them.

The Kerrigans realized after the nocturnal visit of the Simbas, that they were vulnerable. They would come again, and they would search the house. If they found them with the radio transmitter, they would certainly be accused of contacting Belgians and Americans. That would result in a painful execution. While they were "no afraid to die for Chrrrist," they would much prefer it to be in Scotland when it happened. Or better yet, to go up in the Rapture. They waited until the darkness of midnight to go out with pick and shovel and dig a deep hole. They wrapped the equipment in a plastic sheet and ceremoniously, the lovely Scottish couple interred the radio equipment. They even had a committal service, commending the equipment to God, as well as to earth, praying that it would be resurrected when the missionaries came back, and put into use again.

The Kakwa Pastor, Zebadayo, who had been working in Bunia for some years, was also suspect. A unit of soldiers presented themselves at the chapel in the native city. "Where's Pastor Zebadayo?" they demanded.

Zebadayo came out to welcome the Simbas in his usual cordial manner. Cordiality was far from the minds of the sadistic Simbas. They began to beat the dignified greying Pastor with their rifle butts. "You come with us," they commanded, tying his hands behind his back.

They led the old Pastor away. — A scene that must have resembled one that took place in Bohemia about 475 years ago. The Church Council of Constance had been convened by the Roman Catholic hierarchy. Godly preachers like John Hus and his faithful follower, Jerome, were summoned to the Council. Faithful Christians wept as their beloved Pastors were led away to be tried for "heresy", and later to be burned at the stake. Pastor Zebadayo was being led away to be tried.

He was taken to the Bunia prison. A Simba tribunal was set up to give the Pastor a perfunctory trial. "Your name and occupation?"

"I am Pastor Zebadayo Idu, Pastor of Eglise du Christ, Bunia."

"Where did you get your education?"

"On the Mission Station at Adi."

"How long did you work for the missionaries?"

More routine questions were asked, and Zebadayo answered with dignity and forth rightness. He was God's ambassador, and he had nothing of which to be afraid. The interrogator spoke gruffly and with disdain. He was dealing with one of those Pastors who had worked with the hated Americans. One who was certainly a spy for the American

C.I.A.

"Where did the missionaries leave their money?"

"Monsieur, I do not know."

Wham! Across his face came the biting lash of a hippo-hidewhip. Blood spurted from the gash across his cheek. The grey-haired pastor rocked on his heels, but instantly regained his composure. He stood respectfully before his tormentor, ready for more questions and abuse.

"Now, Pastor, if you don't want to see all your blood flowing on the ground like a brook, stop your lying and answer my questions truthfully. Where are the radio transmitters hidden?"

"Monsieur, I do not know," he answered truthfully.

Wham! More lashes on his face, and a rib-fracturing beating that left the Pastor in a state of semi-consciousness. He was dragged to the "cachot", a solitary confinement cell, which was a dark 4' by 5' cell with no ventilation, no furniture, and unbearably hot.

"You will be executed at 5 o'clock this evening," concluded the Simba judge. There were daily executions staged publicly at the Lumumba Monument in the town square. At 5 P.M. Zebadayo was put into a truck with 29 other "criminals", and driven to the "abbatoir" as the Africans called this ghastly slaughtering place. As sheep led to the slaughter, these wretched Africans, most of them fine educated men - the cream of Bunia's crop - were being rushed to their death.

At the town square they were met with a crowd of spectators. The Simbas wanted these executions staged publicly so they could serve as object lessons. A large crowd of Simbas was there, waiting gleefully to see another thriller. They never seemed to tire of seeing human blood flowing down the pavement. That is if it was not their own.

The Simbas in charge were angry. Why had the prison guards dawdled along the way. They were about ready to execute the guards and the chauffeur. The Captain in charge tried to quiet them. "After all," he reasoned, "we must be pragmatic. It's getting late, and it will soon be dark. We must get this job over with so we can get to our feasting and drinking."

"Just a minute," objected one of the executioners, "there are too many. If we kill all 30 of these today, then we may not have any left for a show tomorrow night. We must save some of them for tomorrow night. The Captain pondered the idea. After all, the Simba had a point. "Everybody out of the truck and line up!" barked the Captain.

Poor old Zebadayo was in excruciating pain due to the beating he had received earlier in the day. He managed to let himself slide down from the truck and walk painfully to the end of the line.

"All prisoners count themselves!"

"One, two, three, four," they counted down the line until Zebadayo at the end of the line called "thirty".

"Now" continued the Captain, "all the odd numbers take your places in front of the monument. The even numbers get back into the truck."

Zebadayo, number 30, scrambled back into the truck with the other 14 who had even numbers. These were to go back to the prison to await their doom tomorrow evening. The pastor felt so miserable he wished that he would have had an odd number. He was ready to go home to be with his Lord. But the Russian roulette had cooperated with God's sovereignty. It was decreed that he should live on earth for another 24 hours. Perhaps God had someone to whom Zebadayo was to witness.

The Captain set the stage for the drama. The audience was of a variegated variety. Many were Simbas, in a carnival mood. This was going to be the kind of show they liked most. Many of the audience were Christians who had come, not to see a show, but to pray for Zebadayo in his last moments on earth. Also they wanted to take note of who was being executed so they could bring a report back to the Church.

Some of the spectators were there unwillingly; but forced by the Simbas to witness these daily executions. Any Greek merchants, or others of the Caucasian race who were still in town were told to be there every day. They dreaded the occurrence, but they knew if they absented themselves then they would have to play quite another role in the next day's drama.

The main actors in the cast were, obviously, the hapless and hopeless ones who had been condemned by the Russian roulette. They stood before the monument impatiently, wishing that these stupid Simbas would get the show on the road. They had had enough. Death would be a welcome release, and the sooner the better.

Others in the cast were the 8 Simbas with the machine guns, loaded and ready. The leading actor was the Captain. He was enjoying his role. He had the power of life and death at his command. With a gruesome grin he glared at the condemned men, wondering what it was going to be like for them when he gave the order to mow them down. An emotion of fear gripped him. What if he, the Captain were facing the other way? Could those brave Christians be right after all? About half those to be shot were Christians and not a trace of fear on any one of their faces. The Captain cursed. Those Christians are going to die, and they're not afraid. Actually, they look like they're glad about it.

"Damn!" sighed the Captain, "I envy those Christians". After too long a pause the Captain barked, "Attention! - Take aim! FIRE!"

The firing squad was ready. All together, as though all 8 guns were triggered by one finger, the guns spat out their streams of flaming fire. It seemed that the pit of hell had blown its top. Fifteen pairs of knees buckled. Bodies crumpled. Brave men died at the caprice of the Simbas' Russian roulette. Many spectators burst into tears, and wailing woefully for their fallen neighbors and loved ones.

The group of Christians hurried away from the Abbatoir, back to the chapel, which was packed full. They had been praying for their Pastor until they heard the blasts of the firing squad. Now their leader was in heaven, they thought. Their beloved leader was gone.

When they heard about the Russian roulette they didn't know whether to be glad or sad. Was the 24 hour reprieve on his life worth the discomforts and pain of another night in the "Cachot?"

The Simba leaders were gathered on the other side of the town in what used to be the governor's graceful mansion.

Now it was occupied by the Colonel, and it was a disaster. The filth and smells and disarray were unbelievable. But the Simbas were together with the Colonel for a night of feasting and drinking and riotous living.

"What about Pastor Zebadayo? Was he killed?" the Colonel asked of the Captain. "No, Pastor was not killed. He was an even number. The spirits have decreed that he should live another 24 hours."

The Colonel frowned. It was very plain to see that Zebadayo's God was different; and the Colonel was worried. He didn't mind killing people that belonged to the witchdoctor, but this "Nzambe" and "Yesu Kristu" were something else.

While the Colonel cracked his cranium on the mystery of Zebadayo's God, there was a leader of the women of the church who was praying in her own home for her Pastor. Her name was Cecelia, and she was an important business woman in the town. She had accepted the Lord through the witness of some of the women and through the preaching of Zebadayo. The Simbas respected her, and she was about the only one in Bunia who dared to try to talk sense to the Colonel. She was indignant about the way Zebadayo was being treated. To pray in faith for his deliverance was good, thought Cecelia, but this demanded a bit of works along with her faith. She would put feet to her prayers, and she set her feet in the direction of the Colonel's house.

At the Governor's mansion she was stopped by the guards, but she rolled out her toughest demeanor, and soon had the guards dancing to her drumbeat. She pounded loudly at the door of the Colonel and was soon seated in one of the best chairs in the house.

"Good evening, ma chere Cecelia, What causes you to honor my home with your presence? Is there something I can do for you?" "Yes, Monsieur le Colonel, there definitely is something you can do for me. I think it is despicable the way Pastor Zebadayo is being treated. He is a good man who has never lied to the Simbas. He has given many years of his life to help the black people. You have him in the "cachot", and this morning he was seriously beaten. Tomorrow you are going to have him executed. If you have this man executed, I promise you, the wrath of hell will swallow you up. Zebadayo is a man of Nzambe, and you better reconsider his case."

There was that Nzambe again. Now the Colonel really was scared. What could he do to save face, and also release the man of Nzambe. He hated intensely to show signs of weakness and ambivalence before the Simba leaders. But there was Nzambe.

Hang this business of saving face! "Captain," he called to his officer, "take the limousine and the chauffeur and go to the prison. Have Pastor Zebadayo released to his people. I personally will sign his release paper. Now go quickly and take care of every detail."

"Oui, Monsieur le Colonel," and the Captain was off to do his duty. After midnight the chauffeured Mercedes limo drove up to the chapel with Zebadayo, bathed and fed, sitting beside the Captain.

The Christians were praying still for Zebadayo's release that seemed such a lost cause. They were frightened when the official car drove up. Whom were they going to arrest now?

The car door opened, and out stepped the Captain. The darkness prevented them from seeing who else was in the car. The Captain looked back into the car and spoke gruffly "Toka" (get out).

Out came the Pastor! What in the world was this all about? Zebadayo, smiling broadly, thanked the Captain for his goodness, and the ride. The limousine sped off, and Zebadayo was a free man.

"Will you kindly tell us what this is all about?"

Zebadayo did tell them, leaving out none of the sordid details. The Doxology was sung again and again. Prayers of Praise, and tears of joy bathed their cheeks and the walls of the chapel.

The cocks were crowing again, and the sun was throwing its shafts of light through the Eucalyptus trees. Zebadayo was ready for a new day. He had a prized possession, a letter of release with the Colonel's signature. The Russian roulette had been ruled "out of order" by the sovereign hand of Nzambe.

Cecelia continued to exercise her influence over the Simbas during the four or five months they controlled Bunia. She had a good testimony, and was dearly loved by the Church.

The Central Government finally took control of Bunia Province again. The new authorities heard about Cecelia, and decided that she had collaborated with the Simbas. She was arrested and tried by the legitimate government, and found guilty of treason. She died before a firing squad as crowds of Christians gathered to sing and pray with her, and to mourn her as she left this cruel world. Her "crimes" had been like those deeds she had done to affect the release of her beloved Pastor.

Pastor Yoane stayed in Uganda about three months during the Simbas' occupation of Kakwa land. He ministered to Congolese refugees, and to the Ugandans. Word finally came that mercenary soldiers had quashed the Simba rebellion, and that Kakwa land was free again under the hand of Chief Drupa. Yoane was the first one to go back to Adi to begin the Herculean task of rebuilding the shattered Mission Station. ❖

# World Traveller
# Chapter 19

Yoane was busier than ever during the reconstruction period that followed the evacuations. He was in his sixties and most teenagers had more formal education than he did. He felt that he could not have a ministry among the youth.

Notwithstanding the disparity in age and educational advantages, the young people all regarded Yoane as a great pastor - a man in whom they could confide teenage problems. Yoane became a very popular campus speaker with a remarkable ministry to the students and faculty alike.

The Africa Inland Mission that had been responsible for producing men like Yoane was meanwhile growing up. They started their ministry in 1895 with five missionaries coming to the dark Continent. Growth at first was very slow. After eleven years of heartbreaking, as well as body-breaking ministry, the mission had more missionary graves in Africa than converts. The going was tough and it was very dubious that the mission would survive those early years.

They did survive, however, and in 1970, when Yoane was approximately sixty-five years old, the Mission celebrated its diamond Jubilee. It was to be a great year of setting goals for further expansion into new fields, and greater church growth in the six countries that they occupied at that time. God laid it on the hearts of the International Council members to send several African Pastors to America and Great Britain to preach in the sending churches, and to appeal for more missionaries. They would have to be Pastors who could speak some English, and be educated on the University level. They would have to preach in the great churches of America and Great Britain.

The Mission had some who might meet the educational qualifications, but there was doubt about the spiritual qualifications. Where would they find the right man to send on this Mission? The Council was frustrated.

"Why not send Yoane Akudri?" asked one of the members in desperation. Other Council members smiled at this man's sense of humor. Surely he was joking. Yoane was one of the least qualified. The Councilman who suggested the idea was not joking. He was perpetrating God's sovereign will in this important matter. "Yoane and another one of the "Ordinary" Pastors from another field were chosen to fly to America together.

The Reverend Sidney Langford, our American Home Director wrote to me, asking how both missionaries and the Church would feel about this. We considered it in a joint Church/Mission Council meeting, and there were varied reactions. Some thought it would be very wise; others thought it very preposterous. Some of the African members objected; "Why send Yoane when others among us are so much better qualified?" When the matter was placed before God, and His will earnestly sought, there was unanimity. Yoane would go and the Church would stand with him in prayer. Yoane must be ready in six weeks. This gave us very little time for his passport, and inoculations for yellow fever, typhoid, smallpox, tetanus, etc. Too, there was the matter of his wardrobe. Yoane seldom wore anything but khaki shorts or trousers and a cotton shirt. We had a big job on our hands to get him ready.

He needed a suit. After praying much about this the Lord suggested "Your new Beefeater suit". On our previous furlough I had gone to a Men's shop in search of a good durable furlough suit. Something that I could sleep in while riding in a train, "chair coach".

"I've got just what you need, Pete," said the salesman, showing me a gray "Beefeater". "It's imported, and holds a press very well. In fact, most undertakers in the city buy this suit for their daily use. Not one of the undertakers has ever complained that he looked shabby in the presence of his clients."

That was quite a salespitch, and I wondered how the client could care less whether the undertaker looked shabby or not. His days of being critical were over forever.

The suit looked good nonetheless and I bought it. I had several months of use of it at home before taking it to Africa, where I had only worn it a few times at our General Conference.

Yoane tried on the suit, and he thought it was the best. It fit him very well, except that it was too long for him. Edythe soon fixed that. Our only concern was that Yoane would be taken for the "friendly undertaker". The rest of the wardrobe was soon supplied and Yoane bid us farewell for a trip that would last almost a year. He met the other "ordinary Pastor" from Tanzania in Kampala, and the two of them travelled alone to Nairobi. No language barriers because they could use Swahili.

From Nairobi to England the two Pastors travelled with missionaries going home on furlough. They taught them many things that the sophisticated traveller should know; along with a few English expressions. Yoane already had learned to say, "O.K., O.K." Everything always seemed to be "O.K." with him.

They enjoyed the jet plane very much, although there were too many gadgets and buttons in the restroom. He had learned to flush a toilet back in Bunia, but this "ndako muke" (little-house) was something else. The lock on the door, the toilet paper, the lights all presented problems at first.

Arriving at London Airport the Pastors were met by Joyce and David Richardson. A hilarious welcome took place. Weren't these two Britishers his very own children? Wasn't he there when David made his untimely appearance on the dining room table at his nativity? Hadn't he boiled the milk for Joyce's formulas some 40 years ago? These were his kids and a loud, demonstrative greeting was in order. Never mind the staid and stately British looking on in amazement. He was welcomed into a strange land by his own Kith and Kin.

Yoane's first request was to see the grave of his spiritual father, Ken Richardson, who had died a short time previously. In true Kakwa fashion, he wanted to weep on his grave. For a long time he remained silent, tears dripping on his "Beefeater" suit. Not because his Bwana was dead, did he cry, for he was not really dead. His Bwana was in heaven, but Yoane missed him sorely and unabashedly.

A gang of gravediggers were only a few yards away, excavating another grave. They were amazed to hear Yoane praying "Oh,Nzambe," long pause, and then again, "Oh Nzambe. You remember how this man taught me to pray - Mericee! Mericee!"

His prayer was long and loud. The gravediggers were puzzled. Finally they doffed their hats and stopped their work, and stood with their heads bowed. They didn't understand Yoane's Bangala, but they knew he was talking to God, and that they were on holy ground.

They drove back to the Richardson home in silence. Once there, he said, "Joycee, nzala!" He was hungry. They ate Joyce's tasty meal, and talked about Bwana Richardson.

England was cold, and in spite of the Clothier's remarks about the "Beefeater", he was cold. He needed an overcoat ("great coat") as the British called it.

"We must go to Bwana's bedroom," suggested Joyce. "He has left many clothes. I'm sure we can find something to keep you warm."

There were heavy undergarments, shirts, woolen sox and Yoane was delighted. "Mericee, Mlle Joycie. I will be reminded of Bwana every time I put them on."

There were two heavy "great coats". "Which one would you like, Yoane?"

He tried one on, and it fit him "O.K.". He liked it very much but the other one was just as nice. He tried that on over the top of the first one. It was likewise "O.K." "I like them both, Joycie, May I keep them both? If it's too much for my suitcase, I can wear it."

Joyce, in a fit of laughter, realized that Yoane was not thinking of himself, but many friends at home who would welcome the extra coat. He was assured that he could take both coats.

"But what's a coat without a hat?" added David. "You, Africans, all like to wear a good hat."

There were two hats and the first one fit him well. A mite tight, but it would ride well high on his head. But there were two, and he was thinking of another of his cronies. He placed the second hat on top of the first one. "I can wear them both" said Yoane with deadpan seriousness.

This was a bit much for Joyce. "You may have both hats, but only if you promise me that you'll never wear one on top of the other."

Yoane was well outfitted by Joyce and David. He preached all over Great Britain in Anglican Cathedrals, Baptist, Methodist and Presbyterian Churches, and in many interdenominational conferences. God used him remarkably and many noble and commoner hearts were touched through Yoane's enthusiastic preaching. David did most of the interpreting for him in the Churches, and Joyce in women's groups. His friend from Tanzania was with him all this time, preaching in Swahili. He, too, was very well received.

It was time to go to America. Sid Langford, Peter Stam, Ed Schuit and others met them at J.F.K. Airport. An extensive itinerary had been prepared for the Pastors. The Tanzanian Pastor was whisked off by Swahili speaking missionaries, and Yoane travelled with missionaries who had worked with him in Zaire. The two "ordinary" Pastors proved to be a tremendous blessing in spite of the language barrier.

One of Yoane's meetings was in Florida, where he was to speak to a large group of women. Women who were aristocratic, and of great wealth and sophistication. The auditorium was packed full of notable and beautiful dowagers. Sid and Yoane were seated in plush velour, behind a very intimidating pulpit, waiting to be introduced by an intimidating Pastor. Sid was beginning to wonder if it had been a mistake to invite Yoane to America. What will he say in this awesome situation?

"Yoane, are you scared?" he clandestinely whispered.

"Scared! - Scared of what?" asked the puzzled preacher.

"Look at all those gorgeous gals. Don't they frighten you?"

"Zambi na nini? (why would they frighten me). Bo azi batu te?" (Aren't they people?)

Fear was far from the Kakwa's mind. Simbas had frightened him, and likewise the Belgians. But this array of silk and fluff and color. They were more appealing than appalling. They were a challenge.

"What are you going to preach about?" whispered Sid behind the ramrod back of the Pastor.

"How should I know? God will work."

Sid was scared, looking on the blaze of beauty. There were dazzling chandeliers, painted glass windows, a massive carved pulpit. It was intimidating to Sid, but intriguing to Yoane.

It was time for Sid's apprehension and for Yoane's apathy to cease. They were being introduced by the pompous pulpiteer. What in the world was Yoane going to say?

He flashed one of his broadest smiles, and absolutely dazzled the dowagers from the very start. Then he activated his clarion voice and his vibrant personality.

"Ngai alingi bawasi," started Yoane, and Sid translated, "I am very fond of women". After a dramatic pause he repeated. "Ngai alingi bawasi."

Just what is he leading up to? wondered the women. After another pause, "Why am I fond of women? I like women because they are good cooks."

He went on to tell them of the gourmand delicacies he had been enjoying since coming to America. To the delight of the ladies he explained some of the mysterious works of epicurean delight that emerged out of the beautiful ovens, the microwaves and the grills of his gracious hostesses. As he spoke, he smacked his lips and licked his chops. Most of his audience were culinary experts, and began to plot how they might get this Black preacher to their table.

"I, too, have been a cook," he continued. He went on to tell how he had cooked for Madame Richardson and for Madame Pontier. He told of the sacrifices these women made in order to bring the Gospel to Africa.

"I used to think that our missionaries had so many nice things. Now that I have seen what these ladies give up, I am amazed that they would ever leave all this. But these missionaries tell me that when they consider what our Savior left behind in glory to come to this world to save us, then the price they pay is so pitifully small.

"And I want to thank you beautiful women for your part in sending missionaries to Africa. Had they not come, I and all my people would still be enslaved to the witchdoctor, and to the devil whose servant he is."

He spoke to the women from a warm heart that glowed with the love of Christ. He knew when to quit. "You, white people, are afraid of nothing and slaves to no one. That is almost so. You are very afraid of your watches, and you allow yourselves to become their slaves. God bless you."

He sat down. Sid was no longer worried about what Yoane might say. He had said the right things and even the sophisticated, ramrod back, Pastor was impressed. His message was always fresh and blessedly suited for the occasion. He was asked to preach at the prestigious Park Street Church in Boston by its Pastor, Dr. Harold Ockenga. He spoke at several services, and Dr. Ockenga asked him to share the Sunday morning service. In his short message he told of the most dramatic thing that had ever happened to him. Not of the Simbas, shooting at him as he was perched on the high bamboo platform. Not as he stood before a firing squad. He could have enthralled his audience with such events.

The most dramatic thing he shared with that celebrated congregation was when Bwana Bell came with the gospel. When Ralph and Ellen Davis introduced him to the bleeding Savior that bore his sins' penalties. When the Richardsons, the Pontiers and some of the rest of us came to teach them the rudiments of Bible Doctrine and the ethics of Christian living. He finished his message by making the way of salvation very clear.

The Prince of Pulpiteers, Harold Ockenga got to his feet, "Ladies and Gentlemen," he began, "I have nothing more to say. Yoane has said it all, and the Gospel has been clearly stated. What is good for Africans is good for Bostonians."

He gave a simple Gospel invitation, and a number came to the altar of this historic church to receive the Savior.

Yoane was asked to speak at Moody Bible Institute, and Peter Stam was to interpret for him. Chapel services in such a campus situation can often be devastating for the speaker. It's "par for the course" for the students to go soundly asleep if the speaker is at all ordinary. Dr. Harold Cook led the chapel service. He briefed Peter regarding the format of the service, and cautioned him not to go overtime. Peter Stam, like Sid Langford was a very able interpreter. The students sized up Yoane and decided he was going to be boring.

Yoane expertly sensed the situation and by the time he came to the end of his first sentence, he had his audience's attention. By the end of his first paragraph he had them on the edge of their seat where they sat with eyes glued on Yoane for his whole lecture. When Yoane sat down the whole student body of about 1000 students stood to their feet to give him a resounding ovation. Dr. Cook told Peter, "I have attended these chapel meetings for 25 years. Never have I seen such a response."

He spoke at Wheaton College Chapel and there was a similar response. Dr. Merril Tenny asked him also to speak to a Missions Class. Later he told Peter, "Here at Wheaton we teach a class in Communications. Yoane doesn't need that course."

Wherever he went he was well received, and God used him. His first trip in 1970 was recorded as a great success.

In 1975 A.I.M. became an octogenarian Mission. In view of the success of the first two Pastors' trips, it was decided to send more African Pastors to America. The same difficult decision was faced again - whom shall we send?

There were strong proponents for Yoane going again, and there were others who strongly opposed it. There were those who thought it unfair to some of the others. Again after much prayer, it was decided Yoane should go.

The second tour was even more successful than the first. He was invited to large churches again, like the Church of the Open Door in Los Angeles, The Peoples Church in Toronto, and many more. It was a keen disappointment to me not to be with him on this trip to do some of the interpreting. But that just was not in God's plan.

He came back from his second world tour tired and seventy. It was time for him to slow down a bit. His thrilling world travels were over. He was ready to settle down and be a pastor to his own people.

He was soon back on the trail again - not in a jet liner, but on his bicycle, pushing and pumping it 50 to 60 miles a day. He was up for his prayer time long before the sun was up. By six o'clock in the morning, when the dew was heavy on the foliage, Yoane was ready for his first preaching service. Nobody had ever explained to him what a vacation was. "Vacance" he would ask in French, "Why should I bother with a 'vacance'. The devil never takes one. Why should I?" The next five years were among the most fruitful of his life.

Then came 1980 - another anniversary. Yoane was approaching 75 and he was too old for another transoceanic flight.

God had another plan. Some of the great churches where he had preached before began to ask about the Kakwa Pastor. "When is he coming to America again?" A number of churches asked about him. Once again the subject was on the missions agenda in Pearl River, New York. "Why not?" they asked themselves. They passed the matter to the Central Church Council in Zaire, a body of about 25 black members and 5 whites.

"Yoane go to America again? It isn't fair. Why not send some other Pastor instead?"

It wasn't "fair". The missionaries on the Council were embarrassed. We explained to them that the idea did not generate within the Mission, but it started with a number of Churches in America inviting Yoane specifically. A lengthy palaver pursued.

Etsea Angapoza, Moderator of Zaire's Inland Church, summed up the matter. "My dear brothers, it is my opinion that if the American Churches have been blessed through Pastor Yoane's ministry, and if they are asking him to come, we have no option. Let's send him with our blessing and our prayers."

The speech was met with applause. The septuagenarian saint was soon on his way for a third tour of the Western World. This time there was some frosting on the cake for me when our Home Council asked me to meet him at Denver and tour the Western States with him as his interpreter.

We had our first meeting at Fort Collins. It was a thrill for me to stand beside him and put his message into English. When I introduced him he put his arm around me as he began his message. "Mericee, because you not only sent the old pioneers, but you also sent us younger ones. Like this one who is now acting as my 'interrupter'." He had tried to learn the English word "interpreter" but it always sounded more like "interrupter". The Congregation roared whenever he referred to me as his "interrupter", and a young one in spite of my 70 years.

"When we get to heaven we shall all speak in Bangala", he continued. "Then I won't need Bwana 'Beraseli' (his pronunciation of my name) to interrupt me all the time."

He told about our arrival at Adi in 1940, and how we had started the Bible School there, and how that the Peter Stams and we had engaged in that work for many years. How that he himself had sat under our teaching for 4 years. Later both Joyce and David came back also to Adi to teach in the Bible School.

When his meeting was over Yoane was never at a loss for an appetite. "Nzala, Bwana" (hunger, Bwana). He needed a big meal to sleep on. His first night in Colorado was hot and stifling. Fortunately the motel room was equipped with air conditioning. I turned it up full speed and let the cool air permeate my body. I was sound asleep as soon as we had said our prayers.

Not Yoane - He didn't mind the heat, but the sound of the air conditioner was horrible.

"Bwana", he awakened me, "Turn off that noisy Masini (machine)".

"Oh Yoane, please, it's much too hot if I turn it off."

"Well, its far too cold, and that 'keleli' (noise) won't let me sleep."

Turn it off I did, but I opened the windows wide. By that time it was after midnight, and thankfully, a bit of a breeze. "Hey Bwana! Close the window. That traffic noise chases the sleep away from my pillow."

No air conditioner. No breeze wafting through the window. Now it was my turn to toss around. Yoane was snoring, dreaming about Kakwa land.

At about 4:30 I had drifted off to a sweaty sleep. But it was a plagued sleep. Soon I was awakened with the sound of Yoane's voice. "Oh, Nzambe, Mericee."

Yoane was on his knees beside his bed, pouring out his heart in prayer for his beloved Maria back at Adi. For his wayward sons. How they broke his heart. For all the elders and pastors by name. For his Country - Zaire, was in another political embroglio. He prayed for stability, and a turning to God. Then for the missionaries, "Bless Bwana Beraseli, and Madame Editi." He said some nice things to God about us, and invoked blessing on us. "My 'interrupter' needs help when I preach today. You know, Nzambe, he too is beginning to be a 'mobangi' (old man)." The rascal was at least 5 years my senior.

It was intriguing to lie in bed, listening to him have his rendezvous with God. I got out of my bed and joined Yoane on my knees beside him. We both prayed, and were entranced in the Lord's presence, oblivious to the passing of time. These rendezvous with the Savior became a daily blessed occurrence throughout the weeks we were together.

We finally arrived at Seattle/Tacoma Airport. Edythe was there to meet us. Yoane tossed all reserve to the wind when he saw her. "Oh, Madame Editi", he cried again and again. He had never called her Editi in Africa, but now here on her own turf it was different.

"Editi, sango nini (what's with you), Khah! Khah!"

He was a delightful guest to have in our home for 10 days. He would never think of letting Editi do dishes alone. He paid much more attention to her than to me. The only way I could get at least a small share of the attention was to get a towel and join the dish washing party. The merriment and mirth of this daily celebration became a sacred ritual.

Yoane received a call from the Chairman of the Lions Club (Program Chairman). They wanted him to speak at their luncheon program. I discussed it with Yoane and told him the "Simba Club" wanted him to speak to them. "Are the Simbas here in America too? The last time I saw them they were shooting at me. Why do they want me to come?"

I explained what the "Lions Club" was, and he said "Why not? The Simbas need the gospel too. I'll go and twist their tail this time", he said with a chuckle.

We were seated at the Speakers Table in the beautiful

Everett Yacht Club, where we enjoyed a very fine lunch. "If these lions eat this kind of food, I like them much better than the Simbas we produce in Zaire."

The Chairman of the program was a bit leery. "You know these men are all professional and business men. They represent every kind of religion. Do you think Yoane will say something to offend them?"

I assured the Chairman that Yoane would hold their attention, and that he would not be offensive. I cautioned Yoane, and told him to watch the clock - 1:30 was the quitting time.

"Obangi te" he said to me, meaning "Don't be antsie".

I introduced Yoane to the big shots - several hundred of them, and there was a muffled applause. The doctors, lawyers, judges, teachers, et al settled down for a little "after-lunch" nap. This black character would have nothing to hold their attention.

This was in the spring of 1981. President Reagan had just been shot by a would-be assassin. He had made his first speech after the shooting, while he was still recovering. Yoane had heard that speech.

He began his speech to the Lions. "I love America," he started in Bangala, and I translated it as literally and as realistically as I knew how, trying to interpret not only the message, but also the spirit of Yoane.

"I love your President because he is not afraid to speak what is in his heart. Your President impressed me as a man who loves his Country very much. I heard too that he asked you to pray for him and all the leaders of your Country. I, too, am going to pray for him."

Here he was interrupted by applause. Yoane went on to thank the Lions for America's generous help to Zaire during the Simba events. "Without your help, we would have died. Thank you for the food you sent us when we were starving. Thank you for the medicines you sent us when our own supplies were destroyed by our Simbas. Thank you for the garden tools you sent us when ours were all taken by the Simbas. Thank you Simbas right here in Everett for helping us." Then he turned to me speaking directly to me. "You know, Bwana, these Simbas are gudi (different) than our Simbas in Zaire."

The members were enthusiastic about his message. Again and again they interrupted him with applause. Repeating his last statement again "Thank you, Everett Simbas for helping me personally. When I was a student in the Bible Institute I had a very hard time reading. My eyes were getting tired. I needed glasses. You people sent a big supply of glasses to Bwana Beraseli, and one of those pairs fit me perfectly. I used them for many years."

He had more thanks to express. "Thank you most of all for sending some of your people to be missionaries to us. Had you not done that, I would still be a slave to the witch doctor. But the missionaries taught us the Way of Life."

He went on to give his testimony and the clock was approaching 1:30. "When is this guy going to quit," I worried. The audience, however, sat spellbound, not taking notice of the time.

Yoane hit the high spot of his message and drew it to a dramatic and abrupt close, not more than a minute over-time.

When Yoane sat down the club members arose in unison and gave him a rousing ovation. Everyone seemed very pleased, even the "antsie" chairman smiled at Yoane, and said some nice things about the speaker.

A well-known lawyer got to his feet to speak. "Tell Yoane that he is not through yet. There are some questions we would like to ask. Tell him we'd like to hear about his wife and family.

Yoane told about his wife and children. There were many more questions and it was at least an hour later than the usual closing time when the Chairman interrupted with a question of his own. "What is your speaking itinerary while you are in Everett? Many of us would like to hear you again."

I outlined his schedule, and many of the "Simbas" followed him. His last Service was in the First Baptist Church in Marysville, where I am Associate Pastor. It was on Mother's Day morning and he gave a very appropriate message on Sarah, the Mother of Isaac.

Toward the end of his time in the Northwest he seemed a bit morose. "What's wrong, Yoane? Don't you feel well?"

"I feel fine, Bwana. Only I miss my Maria. I would love to have her with me. I think I should cancel the remaining meetings scheduled for me and go home to her and my family."

The very next day there was a letter from his Maria. "My dear husband," she wrote, "I miss you very much, and would love to have you home. But, Yoane, don't you dare to come back to Africa until you have finished all the work God has for you to do in America. I pray for you many times each day, and spill many tears on my pillow at night thinking of you. But God has a work for you to do and I don't want to see your black face until it's done. I love you, my dear husband, and you may count on it, I'm praying for you." With Love, Maria.

Yoane didn't dare to think about going home until his work was done. That is the story of his life. A wife behind him, and with a stick only if necessary. ❖

1940 - Pete & Edythe (2nd and 3rd from the left) leaving New York with others on their first mission trip to Africa

# *EPILOGUE*

Yoane was the reason for our last trip to Africa several years ago. It was made for the purpose of researching the materials that went into this book. Flying from Nairobi to Bunia in an AIM-AIR Cessna 206 we were warmly welcomed by a large group of Pastors, Church Elders and friends. This was our home turf.

To our amazement Yoane was in the welcoming party. We thought he would have been at Adi, about 250 miles to the North. "Khah, Khah!" he greeted us. "You have come back to Africa to our country to be our missionaries again. You are too young to stay in America. You both still have the bodies of young people."

He failed to notice what Osteoporosis had done to Edythe's back, and that I had developed a "pirate's pot-belly" - that is a "sunken chest".

Yoane, Edythe and I took the little plane the next day to Adi. The landing strip was black with Kakwa and Lugbara people to welcome us home.

"Khah, Khah!", a million of them, it seemed. "Bwana and Madame Beraseli" and their own beloved Pastor Yoane. This called for songs of welcome and blaring trumpets, as well as speeches, and hundreds and hundreds of handshakes. It was "Welcome Home, a'les Kakwas".

We spent two weeks with Yoane from morning 'til night, using a cassette recorder to take his voice home with us, reciting all that had taken place in the preceding chapters. There is far more material than could be profitably used in a book, but I present herewith what has been written. Written not, however, without trepidation. Books are like hiccups. Once they're out, they're irretrievable.

The cornerstone and the capstone of these pages, and all the bricks between, have been laid in the mortar of Paul's statement to the Galatians: "God forbid that I should glory, except in the Cross of our Lord Jesus Christ, by Whom the World is Crucified unto me, and I unto the world." Gal. 2:14. ❖

# Glossary

| | |
|---|---|
| A.N.C.- | Armee Nationall Congolaise |
| Akudri- | latecomer |
| Allah- | Arabic for "God" |
| Aoki kwanza- | Listen to me. |
| apisi ye mwambi- | give him eight |
| Asinziri malamu- | be very careful |
| Askofu- | Bishop |
| Azi kula na yo- | It's your affair |
| Ba Kristu- | plural for Christian |
| bankie- | money |
| basenenes- | farewell greetings |
| bashenzi- | raw pagans |
| Batu Bipuru- | people that are clean of all sin (saints) |
| Batu Mokuru- | |
| Beraseli- | The way the africans pronounced Brashler |
| bibi- | wife |
| bloc- | French idiom for prison |
| buku- | book |
| Bulamatadis- | Belgian officials |
| Bwana- | Master |
| Dabisi- | The way the africans pro `nounced "Davis" |
| Diablo- | Satan |
| fimbo- | whip |
| fufu- | manioc mush |
| fujo- | confused mess |
| gbodi- | bush buck |
| goi- | a native cereal |
| Goliata- | "Goliath" |
| gpedi gpedi- | Cooked greens mixed with lots of ground peanut butter. |
| gudi pinza- | very different |

| | |
|---|---|
| hodi- | doorbell |
| Jaboro- | The enemy of God. (Satan, Devil) |
| jamba- | jungle |
| Kakwas- | Kakwa tribe of which Yoane was a member |
| Kapita- | leader |
| kataras- | tennis shoes |
| kebukebu- | leprosy |
| keleli- | noise |
| Khah- | exclamation of delight |
| kitipalas- | small foot stools |
| Kitoko- | The beautiful one |
| koko- | chicken or rooster |
| konyuke- | a soft wood native tree |
| Kristu- | Christ |
| Kula azi te- | no affair |
| kwanza te- | not yet |
| Kuna na ngambo- | across that next stream |
| laisser-passer- | permits to leave the country |
| libanda- | court yard |
| likondos- | evil spirit |
| Lora- | heaven |
| M'zee- | respectful title for "old man" |
| macaque- | monkey |
| mai- | water |
| maimisu- | water of the eyes (tears) |
| malamu- | O.K. |
| manioc- | flour made from casava root |
| masanga- | beer |
| masini- | machine |
| mbote- | greeting "hello" |
| mbote mingi- | a very good evening |
| mbudu- | valley |
| merci mingi- | thank you very much |
| Mite- | a subchief who lived near the Nzoro river. |
| mobangi- | old man |
| mondeles- | white men |
| mondeli asirayii- | White man has arrived. |

| | |
|---|---|
| Monganga- | medical doctor |
| Monoko na Nzambe- | Word of God |
| Mototo na Yawili- | The child of mischief |
| mwana- | child |
| mwasi- | wife |
| ndako muke- | little house |
| ngambo- | across the riverites |
| Ngange na Bashenzi- | Witch doctor |
| nyama- | animal |
| nzala- | hunger |
| Nzambe- | El Sheddai - Almighty God |
| Nzambe azi, Ye Akuki- | God is alive, and He will help you. |
| nzenzes- | native guitars |
| obangi te- | "don't be antsie" |
| Oyo-azi nini?- | What is this? |
| pembe- | A white mud found in stream beds and used for white wash on a building. |
| pikipiki- | motor cycle |
| pitaro- | hospital |
| posho- | food ration |
| purupuru- | diarrhea |
| Risisi- | the way the africans pronounced "Richardson" |
| Sango Malamu na Yesu- | The Gospel of the Lord Jesus |
| Sango nini?- | How are you? |
| sopo- | stomach or inside |
| sufu- | chicken gravy |
| tangba- | drums |
| Tata- | Yoane's uncle |
| tepoy- | carrying chair |
| toka- | get out |
| toli- | rule |
| uhuru- | swahili for freedom |
| unijambiste- | one legged |
| unimog- | tractor-truck vehicle |
| vacance- | vacation |
| wapi- | nothing doing |

| | |
|---|---|
| waraga- | letter |
| yawili- | mischief |
| Yoane- | John |
| Yesu Kristu- | Jesus Christ |
| Zambi na Oyo- | "because of this" |
| Zande- | Chieftainship - or the original Chief Zande |
| Zeriba- | Girls' School Compound |